Morning,

Noon, and

Night

ALSO BY JUDY COLLINS

*Sanity & Grace: A Journey of Suicide,
Survival, and Strength*

Trust Your Heart

Singing Lessons

Shameless

Voices

Amazing Grace

The Judy Collins Songbook

Morning,

Noon, and

Night

Living the Creative Life

Judy Collins

Jeremy P. Tarcher / Penguin

a member of Penguin Group (USA) Inc., New York

JEREMY P. TARCHER/PENGUIN
Published by the Penguin Group
Penguin Group (USA) Inc., 375 Hudson Street, New York, New York 10014, USA •
Penguin Group (Canada), 10 Alcorn Avenue, Toronto, Ontario M4V 3B2, Canada (a division
of Pearson Penguin Canada Inc.) • Penguin Books Ltd, 80 Strand, London WC2R 0RL,
England • Penguin Ireland, 25 St Stephen's Green, Dublin 2, Ireland (a division of
Penguin Books Ltd) • Penguin Group (Australia), 250 Camberwell Road, Camberwell, Victoria
3124, Australia (a division of Pearson Australia Group Pty Ltd) • Penguin Books India Pvt Ltd,
11 Community Centre, Panchsheel Park, New Delhi–110 017, India • Penguin Group (NZ),
Cnr Airborne and Rosedale Roads, Albany, Auckland 1310, New Zealand (a division of Pearson
New Zealand Ltd) • Penguin Books (South Africa) (Pty) Ltd, 24 Sturdee Avenue,
Rosebank, Johannesburg 2196, South Africa

Penguin Books Ltd, Registered Offices:
80 Strand, London, WC2R 0RL, England

Most Tarcher/Penguin books are available at special quantity discounts for bulk
purchase for sales promotions, premiums, fund-raising, and educational needs.
Special books or book excerpts also can be created to fit specific needs. For
details, write Penguin Group (USA) Inc. Special Markets, 375 Hudson Street,
New York, NY 10014.

An application has been submitted to register this book with the Library of Congress.
ISBN 1-58542-415-3

Printed in the United States of America
1   3   5   7   9   10   8   6   4   2

This book is printed on acid-free paper. ♾

BOOK DESIGN BY CHRIS WELCH

A list of permissions appears on page 187.

All this made me start wanting . . . to be artistic, a free spirit, and yet also to be the rare working-class person in charge of her own life.

—Anne Lamott, *Bird by Bird*, 1994

Thanks

They say that gratitude is the aristocrat of the emotions, and I am grateful to many people in my life for their gift of process. We all need people to teach us and we all need to teach, and today I give thanks to the people from whom I have learned much about creativity: my mother and father, who gave me by their example the work ethic that drives my days and the appreciation for literature and art that is the foundation of all my efforts to live the creative life; to Louis Nelson, my husband; to Joel Fotinos, who understands; to the *Sullivanians,* who were my therapists in the years in which I was battling my demons, fighting to find a way to be creative—my twenties and early thirties, the years of trial and error, of tears and suicidal thoughts—and all my other therapists; Ira Progoff, great teacher and founder of *Dialogue House,* where I had great break-throughs in my late forties; to my first work group, which I started with Susan Crile, the painter, and Cynthia Macdonald, the poet, in a time of rich exploration and of important song-writing; to my current writing coach, Jerry Mundis, who has written inspiring books about creativity; to my friend Julia Cameron, who wrote *The Artist's Way,* a book that has inspired millions of creative people on their journeys; to my friend the brilliant writer Susan Cheever, who reads everything I write and lends me her enormous insight and support; to Anne La-mott, whose fine book *Bird by Bird* reminds us that to be con-scious is an art; and to every writer who has contributed to *Writers at Work,* the great collection of writers' stories of how they work; to Flannery O'Connor, whose collection of letters, *The Habit of Being,* was the companion on my journey from songwriting to writing prose, in my mid-thirties and early for-ties; thanks to Al Lowman, my agent; to Katherine De Paul, president of my record label; to Bridget Maybury; and to every artist who has talked to me about their process; every artist who has said nothing; often, silence can be powerful. I am grateful for all their help and confidence in the powers of process in me, since I, like most, have often had enormous doubts.

Thank you.

To Hollis, my granddaughter, and
Louis, my husband,
and my beloved family

Contents

Night

Morning,

Noon, and

Night

Introduction

Creating is what we all are doing, even when we don't know it, all the time, all our lives. To live the creative life is to *notice*. But every day we face the questions and the problems of creativity, as well as the joys. Creativity is a heavenly place to be, but what price do we pay to get here, and what to stay here?

In this book I share my experience with those who are just

starting out, and those, like me, continuing on this path. I discuss the difficulties of staying on the path. I talk not only about writing books and music, which are the primary things I do with my creative time, but the many things *you* might be doing that could benefit from this morning, noon, and night approach. You may be writing a book of recipes, with memories woven between the stories of what you like to eat, what interested you at a particular time in your life.

Perhaps you are a clothing designer, a composer, a choreographer, a painter. You might be a playwright. Music, dance, literature, all take form and substance, and discipline. For any discipline you might be interested in pursuing, there is inspiration to be found all around us in every instant of our lives!

There is a feeling of early summer in the air today, cool air, and the wind moving through the trees. The Hudson ripples in light outside my window. I feel rested and ready to go on this Monday morning, my favorite time to start new projects, to get my engine in gear, as my father would say—to continue to spin this web of beauty in which I live and work, thrive and dream.

When I was young, and another school year was about to start in September, I always felt that heartening of spirit—new pencils, erasers, and a good stout ruler of bright-colored plastic. Notebooks, a list of the books I would have to read for my classes—math, English, geometry, drama, music; the new teachers, the new ideas, the subjects I would take on that I had never thought much about. I had a happy feeling in my heart, one that said I could do this.

I've been out of school for many years now. A professional as well as a dreamer, an artist as well as a friend and wife, family member and concert artist, but I know I will always be a student, that I love to learn, and learning new things keeps me alive.

○

I have been, for much of my life, a person who doesn't feel something has really happened until I have written or sung about it.

I didn't write songs until I was in my mid-twenties, but my heart yearned, sought, wept, bled, even, to BE a creative person. I sang, I played the piano, and wanted more than anything in the world to be an artist, to create beauty, to live and walk and breathe in beauty. I could see no other means of my own salvation. To suffer, perhaps! Always to suffer. But what pleasurable suffering!

I need to create to be truly alive. And I have come to believe that many of us have that drive, that hunger, that love of beauty. It is just a question of where to look, what to do with all that eager joy, the feelings I felt when I was fifteen.

In my home there was a constant thread of creativity going on, from morning till night, the day starting with a fine breakfast made by my mother, bacon and eggs and French toast if we were lucky, and fruit cocktails. My father's voice would boom out of the bathroom, or the bedroom, where he warmed up his voice for the songs he would sing on the radio. Daddy had a radio show from 1937, in Seattle, where he started broadcasting on a local radio station, singing his songs, those he wrote and those he loved, to the last years of his life in Denver, when he died in 1968. As children, all of us listened to him warm up in the morning and do his radio shows when we were not at school, and accompanied my parents when Daddy sang at fundraisers and events in the cities in which we lived—Seattle, Los Angeles, and Denver.

When my father came to the breakfast or the dinner table, he would try out his poems and quotes and jokes on all of us, having written them out on his Braillewriter, for himself, and the typewriter, so that his recording and broadcast engineers would have a copy of the show to follow along with. "Grab your coat and get your hat, leave your worries on the doorstep," he would sing, and then reveal to us that the song was written by a woman (Dorothy Fields, one of the only women writing popular songs in those years) and a woman was as good as a man. Often better, he told us. He would extol my mother's gifts as a cook and as a seamstress and, though he had never seen her because he was blind, as a beautiful woman.

My father would also tell us how fortunate we were, with the delicious meals that Mother cooked, and the beautiful

clothes she made for us and our good minds and good education. He urged us to be grateful for our good fortune. He treasured the life he had hewn out of hard work and advised us that
hard work would pay off for us, as it clearly had for him, a blind
boy from a farm in Idaho who would hardly have been a safe
bet for becoming a breadwinner with a successful, creative career, a growing family, and a fulfilled, happy life.

And so, in this home of good food and good music and the
buzz and hum of a life filled with books and trips in the car and
parents who filled out in each other what the other lacked, I
must have felt that creativity was an integral part of life, not
something separate from it. However, this is not to say that life
was perfect. But while my parents might rail at each other,
fighting like the cats in the backyard at times, they always settled back into their lives, raising their five children, reading
books, making meals, singing songs, and laughing a good deal.

Perhaps the laughter was pure gold, for we never had much
fortune but through the industry of our creativity—the poems
we wrote for our Christmas cards, the laughter we experienced
over a family meal, telling each other what we had done, who
we had seen, what the world had brought to our door. Sometimes there were potential disasters that turned into the stuff of
the family legends, such as when Daddy, who loved nothing
more than to go out on a crisp Colorado morning and start the
car (whether it was the Buick or the Dodge, or, later, the English Rover; he loved to listen to the motor purr, "warm it up

for you, Marjorie"), pushed the wrong pedal and ran the car through the front end of the garage, scattering mortar and bricks all over the backyard. Sometimes there was chaos in his energy, but how he loved to rev up his engine, to get going! I hope I will always love to rev up my motor, to revel in that sort of childlike energy, our own pure gold, not fortune, but fortunate.

I took out my journals for the past few months so I can look at them and find out if I have written things down that may help me start writing about creativity—sayings, quotes from newspaper articles, poems I have finished. To maintain my creative energy I am always learning, listening, hoping that the world around me will teach me something new.

I contemplated writing this book about the creative life with a great deal of joy. It gives me a chance to break down my process and share it with others, to look at how what I do on a daily basis has formed the life I lead, which is a life of singing, writing song and books, and touring many weeks out of the year. I can learn how I am living with the ups and downs of taking the risk of living out my wildest dreams.

☽

I have divided this book into three sections: Morning, Noon, and Night, since I believe the truly satisfying creative life has to be led not one book or record or song at a time, but one day at a time. In each part of the day, I focus on different things. In the morning there is celebration, which for me involves gratitude and wonder at the day and the things I am blessed with; starting, getting the fresh creative work done while I am totally alert. Remembering and reading are also part of the morning practices that help me.

At noon I treat myself well, have a nourishing lunch alone or with friends. The afternoon is for many things—rewriting, polishing, and releasing. The afternoons are also for those things we all need—appointments with the foot doctor, taking the visiting niece to lunch, having our hair done (or in my case colored)—on a regular basis. I believe a truly creative and satisfying life is a balance of work and trips to the museum, delicious meals, long talks with friends and relatives, and eight hours of sleep, which brings us to night.

Night blooms with hoping and imagining, praying and forgetting, and resting, so that the deep healing of sleep can restore us. I need eight hours of sleep, and often find that ten on a weekend is just the right amount.

Then I see that I get my proper share of reading, movies, walks, visits, and museums! I don't talk about vacations or weekends off in the book, but I have found that to give myself the proper rest and change of emotional scenery, I must take a couple of two-week vacations a year, and find at least one day a week as well and one weekend a month where I really do not work, but read, go to movies, take walks, visit with friends and family, see theater, go to museums, and even, heaven forfend, do nothing!

But it is the small things that get the Creativity flowing—the smell of new paper, clean sheets, the wind on a September day, the crack of a book as I open it on a fresh subject, that I find the most thrilling.

—*Judy Collins*
New York City
September 2004

Morning

Celebrating

The consolation, the dignity, the joy of life are that discouragements and lapses, depressions and darknesses come to me only as one stands without—I mean without the luminous Paradise of art. As soon as I re-enter it—cross the threshold—stand in the high chamber, and the gardens divine, the whole realm widens out again before me and around me—and the air of life fills my lungs—the light of achievement flushes over all the place, and, I believe, I see, I do.

—Henry James, *The Other House*, 1896

*W*hen I begin my creative session in the morning there are things I like to have to make me feel like celebrating—a flower in a crystal bowl, perhaps a sweet bell or the resonating bowl and clapper from Tibet, the singing sound that fills the room and brings me calm, and gratitude for all there is in my life. On my table there will be a notebook for my dreams and journals, a lamp—a pretty one, perhaps of colored glass. On my chair or my bed will be a pillow for meditation. I suggest everyone keep a notebook for writing dreams and thoughts and keeping track of all the things that are going on in our lives. Even writing for ten or twenty minutes a day can set us on the path.

Celebration could include:

- Dreaming
- Visualizing
- Making lists
- Planning like an architect
- Letting go like a sky-jumper!

The celebration of life begins for me when I wake, often at dawn in some city on the road. I try to think of the positive first thing in the morning, count my blessings, and celebrate the good things in my life. Difficulty is part of all our lives, but the moment of awakening is a time for rejoicing and celebrating that here we are, one more day, grateful and alive and ready to begin anew, in a fresh day that holds promise no matter what. Our own new beginning, every day.

I found my first voice very early on, in music. Singing came naturally to me. I can open my mouth and sing now, anytime, anyplace, day or night, rain or shine, as Max my teacher of thirty-two years taught me to do. Also, I have discovered a number of other voices, some of them easier for me to express than others.

When I am writing, singing, practicing the piano, working on a song, writing in my journal, or painting a watercolor, I am never tempted to be negative. For some reason, my spirit is lifted by the positive energy I get from every creative aspect of my "voices," and no negativity can interfere, as I float in the atmosphere of "doing" and "being" at the same time. I fly, with the wings of the work, of the thought.

Emmet Fox says that God is where the problem exists, and when you think of God, or light, as some say, you cannot think of the problem. So—no negativity! The problem is to get into the light, and out of the dark, and creativity works wonders for that part of my life. Creativity pays off in clarity of thought, as well as in the beautiful thing I may be able to create.

I wrote my first journal in 1955, when I was sixteen. I still have it, dog-eared, its pencil-written pages filled with crossed-out events, things I really didn't want anyone else to know about—the dates, the feelings, ugh, that kiss! Dreamy, that kiss! Not being asked to the Sweetheart Dance, *being* asked to the Sweetheart Dance! And dancing like a robot, really being dragged over the dance floor by my handsome, impeccably dressed date, the beautiful Randy Robinson, who lived down the street and, after that night, would never ask me on a date again. But oh, the memory! I couldn't really dance, to be sure, but on that night, I was close to heaven.

It seemed to me that I had to write in my journal and sing and create in order to make the events of my life, like that dance with Randy, real. And to find out what was really going on in my family, in my world. It was a world in which there were secrets and pitted, dark places that I was afraid of falling into. Making something out of nothing put on the light.

Daddy taught me the first lessons of creativity—to be joyous, to celebrate. He and my mother gave me the feeling that living a creative life was a necessity.

I often reach for the connection to creativity that began in my childhood—and the connection to people who are no longer here with me. They inform the paintings I do and the prose I write that are all a kind of swirling field of light and beauty that surround me.

One winter day a few years ago I sat upstairs writing in my ever-present notebooks, doing my morning journaling. My mind came to rest on the idea of the fallow time of year, when the crops are let to rest and the earth to heal. It makes me restless sometimes, this strangely quiet time between seasons, between bursts of activity. And to express that feeling I began to write what I thought was a poem, and later turned it into a song.

I'll learn to love the fallow way
When winter draws the valley down
And stills the rivers in their storm
And freezes all the little brooks

Time when our steps slow to the song
Of falling flakes and crackling flames
When silver stars are high and still
Deep in the velvet of the night sky

The crystal time the silence times
I'll learn to love their quietness
While deep beneath the glistening snow
The black earth dreams of violets
I'll learn to love the fallow way

You have to take in the weather, the snow, and the hot sun, remember to celebrate even the fallow times. And when you don't know how to find your way out of the dark nights, to

Simply stay in the battle of leading a creative life,
no matter what.

And so, as I learn to celebrate what is good and positive and wonderful in my life, counting my blessings and looking for the inspirations that are all around me every minute of each day, I begin to find what it is that I want to create out of the light and out of memory, out of my dreams, and out of thin air.

You, too, can do this, as your celebration
becomes tangible.

Chapter 2

Starting

There's a time that comes once every morning
When you choose the kind of day you will have
It comes in with the sun and you know you've begun
To live the life you dream
You can light all your candles to the dawn
And surrender yourself to the sunrise
You can make it wrong you can make it right
You can live the life you dream

Pray to Buddha pray to Krishna pray to Jesus
Or the shadow of the devil on your wall
Anyone you call . . . will come . . .

      —Judy Collins, "The Life You Dream," 1983

I clear the decks,
I clean my room,
I put away the things that have been out here for weeks, or months—
I dust things off,
I clear off my work spaces,
I close off the room from interruptions—
I light a candle,

I ring the little bell,
I gaze at the small stone, the glass paperweight,
    the soft petals of the flower—
I meditate for at least ten minutes,
Now I am ready.

T he vessel of creativity is the day. Creativity is held in every day in even the smallest things.

Coffee. Designer protein. Whole-grain toast. I Can't Believe It's Not Butter! Part-skim cheese.

The vessel is sometimes *not reading the paper* before I go to work, not allowing my imagination to have some time to breathe.

The vessel is *meditating, being silent. Being alone.* Knowing that I am going to spend an hour this morning writing, then another working on the piano and on songs.

The vessel is the *desk, the piano, and the blank paper. The candle.*

It is knowing I will see good friends, talkative, bright, interesting friends later in the day.

After the work I do today.

Whatever the day brings is part of my creativity. The people I talk to, the books I read. The paintings I look at, the air I breathe. The dreams I have, the hopes I hold. The mistakes I make. The meals I eat, the meals I miss!

The vessel of creativity is setting aside time to work. The vessel is the phone I let ring, the door I close, the candle I light, the river out the window, the dreams that hover after I wake from my blessed sleep, sleep that is often filled with dreams. It is the phone call I answer; it is the telephone call I *don't* answer.

Now, you may be saying to yourself:

> *"This is all well and good for someone who has no family to cook for, no children to shepherd to music lessons and school, no family to focus on!"*

But the creative life is all of these things. It is family, obligations, and pressures of health and demands that our society and our own consciousness make upon us. Still in the midst of all of this, there is always the small voice that calls to us—to paint, to write poems, to sing, to learn to play the bass.

⁂

My foot doctor, who is in his late fifties, is just beginning his lessons on the bass guitar. He feels it will give his life more meaning, and whether it is the bass guitar or some other creative outlet, the need calls, the urge is there in most of us, and we just have to find the time to do the things that will make the quality of our lives better—to do something artistic to nurture our souls. And there is a way!

*The best advice, give or take, has always been
to follow your heart, your eye, to go with what
moves you, what gives you pleasure.*

And in that desire, to do something, make something, is our destiny as creative people. Anything can get me started in the morning when I go to my piano, or my desk, or into the recording studio. The inspiration can be the beauty of the day and the way the light comes into my windows, the way the rain falls and the sun shines, the way my face feels in a clean wind that blows off the river; part of the day, and the life, and the moment.

Over the years I've developed a specific way to get started. Your way will be different, but over time you will find your own way to begin. Just try different things until you figure out what works best for you. I have learned that the best way to get to my creative sessions is to put on makeup, dress, brush my teeth, have my coffee or muffin, or oatmeal; or Slim-Fast!

I take all the photos off the mirror and the notes and the *New Yorker* cartoons off the glass door of my shelves.

The night before, I put most of the watercolors I have done

this year away. I leave one painting tacked in the middle of my painting wall so that, before I go to sleep, I can see it as I turn out the light. In the dark it still glimmers, and perhaps it will bring me a fine new dream. I take most of them off the wall and put the color-tipped tacks in a miniature Acoma bowl, made somewhere in New Mexico. The design of the inch-and-a-half-wide bowl is tiny and specific, made by the hand of someone who knew making beauty in a day is making the day live, somehow, forever. In the bowl there is beauty, in the vessel that is the day there is calm and I am ready to work.

The wall is ready for the next group of paintings.

This is a day I will create something of beauty.

I have learned that if I have a writing or creative block, I have to start slow in the beginning.

If you're suffering from a block I recommend you work for only fifteen or twenty minutes, then go on with your day. The next day, increase your time, and as the week and the month progresses, move up to the time you want to work each day.

Before you know it, you will be doing an hour a day, which is probably enough to get a good deal of work done.

You will add the time you need to rewrite and to polish, to think about other projects, outside of this hour, but keep the hour sacred. And continue to do this religiously, each day, five or six days a week.

*On the Sabbath, one day out of seven, a day of
your choice, you might want to take the day
off for all the other things that feed
creativity, including rest.*

There are tools, rules of the game, if you like.

One is consistency.

The best method I have found is to get up at about the same time every day. I find the morning is best for me, but find what works for you. I get up on the early side, hit my knees and pray for courage! And for anything else that strikes my fancy. I read a few of my books of meditations as well as some poetry, perhaps some Emmet Fox. I am reading a book now called *The Mind on Fire,* the life of Ralph Waldo Emerson. He is constantly inspiring.

*I moved my coffeemaker into the bedroom so that I
don't even have to leave the bedroom to
have coffee and start work.*

After meditation and coffee and perhaps writing in my journal, I go to work. I will have finished off as much busy work and business the night before, and cleared my desk of everything I can.

I usually light a candle and get to work, for an hour or perhaps two. The dream from the night before may be hovering in my consciousness, which is the reason I try not to leave my room before I work. There is a precious sort of presence that is neither waking nor sleeping that I find promotes what I call "automatic" writing, where I am not really conscious of what is coming out, and later, am surprised, and sometimes pleased, at what the Great Presence has given to me.

In this process of making "something out of nothing" we are often crafting a web of certainty to house the uncertainty of life.

I have found that meditation is another important part of getting started for me. Meditation allows me to do the things I could not have thought possible. If I meditate before I work, I will often get to things I had not dreamed of. Ideas will spring into my head as though through divine intervention.

People have been doing meditation in many different forms for centuries. Try finding your own way. You might want to follow your breath, or say your favorite prayers silently or aloud. You may read the Bible and concentrate for a few moments on the flame of a candle. You might want to make up your own mantra, bringing all your dreams into your mind and life, asking whatever Power you believe in to help you make them come true.

Any kind of meditation is fine. You will get the guides you ask for.

In my own practice, which has evolved over time, I affirm that every day is an opportunity to understand that I am part of something of inconceivable size, of unimaginable power, and of limitless knowledge. That knowledge, that power, that force, are all inside me, and if I can connect even for a moment to that great power, I can see my way.

For me, *time is the disciplinarian of creativity.* Meditation gives me that connection. I use a little bit of every day to work toward creating something that will fulfill my heart's desire. But I rarely use the whole day.

When I was young and frantic, and less disciplined, or perhaps just very excited and less prepared, I used to work for hours on a song or a project, staying up all night, wearing myself out, getting ill from worry and lack of sleep. I would allow other people to dictate my work schedule, recording at night, or rehearsing in the early evening instead of in the morning, when my creative clock is better adjusted and I can do more with less energy. I used to burn all my candles at every end.

I try mostly not to do that anymore.

It is important to find the time that is best suited to your own inner creative clock. I usually don't work past two in the afternoon, even when I am trying to finish something. I will, though, on occasion, work all day for days if I am in the editing and cleaning-up process, near to publication of a book, or near finishing up a new album. But it is not the same frantic and exhausting process it used to be. Today I gauge my energy and make sure I get all the things I need into my day, along with my work.

I try not to judge as I work at something. The critic will come soon enough, to the show, to review the record, to view the paintings; and I myself will become a judge of what I am doing, but that happens later, after a good chunk of work is done and there is something under my hands to shape and to refine. I like "shape and refine" better than "judge." *Sometimes my opinion is none of my business,* even of what I think is the best or the worst of my work. The important thing is to get it done. As someone said, anything worth doing is worth doing badly! If I were to judge everything as I go along, I would most likely hang up my pen in despair!

Everyone has habits of work that form over time. I began my training as a pianist when I was five, so I learned that a certain amount of time every day has to be committed to practicing scales, memorizing new material, and working up the existing pieces so that they could be performed. It all takes time.

When we are in the creative flow, when time seems to stand still for hours during a day, or just for that hour or two when we are working—when the flow takes over and the mind is freed, when the heart is steadied and that glow comes from within and takes over without, what a glory it is!

I need nothing but this creative flow, these hours, alone, with my thoughts, my books, my notes, my memories, my music, my glances forward, and back. My heart is meant to do these things.

Be in the present, for we know this is all there is.

P eople often ask me how I choose the songs I sing. There are deep creative reasons for the choices each of us makes. The answer to the question of why I choose one song over another is also the answer to every question of creativity: you do what you love, what moves you, what you feel you are called to do.

Songs come to me in mysterious ways. The first songs I learned were the lullabies my mother and father sang to me, songs that stayed in my blood with a force; primal stories and melodies. *Hush, little baby, don't say a word. / Papa's gonna buy you a mockingbird.* My mother sang a song that started:

I've a dear little dolly
She has eyes of bright blue
She can open and close them
And she smiles at me too
In the morning I dress her
And she goes out to play
But I like best to rock her
At the close of the day

Just humming the melody and hearing the words to that little lullaby brings back the smell of my mother's cologne, her face bent low over mine in my soft, warm bed, her silk scarf brushing my face as she left me to go out with my father for the evening. "Now behave," she would say as she finished the song, and I would flutter my eyelids and pretend that I would. But I couldn't do anything else; her voice had soothed me to sleep and I was safe again, for the night, in my bed, having been sung to sleep. There is nothing like that, being sung to sleep.

Songs I learned in camp still evoke the golden leaves of the aspen turning in late August in the mountains. And the songs I learned when I was working on a dude ranch in Colorado and sang with my sister-in-law Hadley can still bring me the sound of a rushing river under the hooves of my saddle horse, crossing a creek overflowing with white sparkling bubbles and adolescent, romantic dreams. There were the English and Scottish rounds learned from my friends the Fletchers in our nights around a roaring fireplace at the Fern Lake Lodge in Rocky Mountain National Park, our singing voices sailing out over the dark forests and the still silvery lake outside under the stars, a million miles from roads and crowds, from concert tours and lonely nights in lost hotels on the road. Peace, serenity, friendship, all in a song.

I learned songs from the radio. I fell in love with the ballad of Barbara Allen when I first encountered folk music; the songs my father sang on his radio show still send chills down my spine—"Where or When," "April in Paris," "When We Were Seventeen," sung by Frank Sinatra and rolling over the rainy mountainsides out the window of Beaver Lodge in Winter Park; Hank Williams songs played on a jukebox at a roadside diner named Wally's where I danced cheek to cheek with a bellyful of three-point-two beer.

Every song that ever took my heart had a special piece of my heart already in it, whether it was "Marieke" by Jacques Brel or "Both Sides Now" by Joni Mitchell; "Maid of Constant Sorrow" by anonymous or Billy Joel's "New York State of Mind," which I have never recorded but plan to someday.

And then there are my own songs, in which I have to play very different roles. First that of the writer, so that I craft a song that works, and then the singer, so that the song fits me there, too. The thoughts come to me for songs when I am noodling at the piano, letting my fingers find the melody and my voice find the words.

Also, there are certain images I draw on when I begin a work session, memories and mantras to get the writing started—

The face of a deer; water, in streams and rivers, running through green trees, bouncing and singing over rocks; tumbling down the mountain side. I think of water skipping, sliding, and dancing. It's the rocks in the river that make the river sing.

A train whistle, loud and clear that sounded from the window of a motel in Washington State. It was night, and I looked out the window and saw the moonlight on the landscape and the mountains and heard the train whistle and knew it was very near.

I was asked once to write a song for a movie called *Table for Five*, starring Jon Voight. It was a story in which a divorced mother of four young children is killed in a car accident and her husband, their stepfather, has to make peace with the children's birth father, and find a way to include him in their upbringing.

I saw in the song, which would play at the end of the movie, a conjunction of the sun and moon in the sky at the same time, from which came the images for the lyrics. These two men had no road map to follow. They had to follow their hearts, and I called the song "Trust Your Heart."

The song was used in the Japanese version of the movie, and with the song included, the movie was a big hit. It was not used in the States, where it wasn't a big hit. I'm not sure if the song made the difference, but, in private moments, I like to think it did!

And I have to laugh at myself, for who knows? What does one good song do for the world? That is the question, and I am always going to try to prove it makes a great deal of difference. Even if it doesn't, I am going to keep believing that it does. For, if nothing else, if one song touches one individual life, then it is a worthy effort.

In the sky the phantom moon appears at midday
To join the sun in some forgotten dance

In their light our voices tremble with reflections
Of what we know and what we leave to chance
The heart can see beyond the sun
Beyond the turning moon
And as we look
The heart will teach us
All we need to learn
We have dreams
We hold them to the light like diamonds
Stones of the moon and splinters of the sun
Some we keep
To light the dark nights on our journey
And shine beyond the days that we have won
The heart can see beyond our prayers
Beyond our fondest schemes
And tell us which are made for fools
And which are wise men's dreams
Trust your heart
Trust your heart

And so, the day begins, and I start the process by which the engine of the creative juices can flow, in which I can be happy and productive, and give my day the balance, the fulfillment, and the shape that will take me through to what I intend to do and say, to be and to create. From the moment I rise and start, the celebration flows. Anything may come my way during the day, and I hope and pray that I use it well, not expecting too much or too little, and thinking always of how the beauty around me inspires me to think and act. To be alive is to start each day in a new way, each moment in a new thought. Each time I work I draw from the connection between my life and the universe. Inspiration is everywhere I look, in the good and the bad, and sometimes the darkness leads to a new light.

I await the dawn, to start the celebration.

Chapter 3

Disciplining

The night comes to you dressed in darkness
Descends on your body like a blessing
You can lie in its arms it will heal your heart
You can live the life you dream
You can wake in this vale of tears
You can laugh like a child again
You can make it right you can make it wrong
You can live the life you dream
What you see and you believe is not the answer
To anything that matters very much
Anything you touch . . . is gone—
    —Judy Collins, "The Life You Dream"

Sometimes it does not come easily, this process of creativity. Even doing the things that we love takes hard work.

I am finally home from the road for a few days, and hope to open up the dialogue with my writing again, with my new album, for which I have to finish and organize some songs. I seem to have floated into a kind of fog of not working, but reading, socializing, working on the road doing concerts, visiting with family and friends at home. I seem to be on strike as far as my creativity goes.

Each day, even with a strong discipline and a sense of where I am going and what I have to do to get there I have to begin anew, and create from a place of healed wounds. I know this malaise will only be cured by the discipline I have fought to incorporate into my life.

The word "discipline" has always fascinated me. The root is the word "disciple," which means to follow a master.

> *Who is your master?*
> *Who makes the rules?*
> *There are no experts.*
> *Except you.*

No career success ever has the perks that one imagines when one is growing up, when one has not experienced successes, or fame. The lessons come with time, and the truth is that creativity is necessary to live; but success is not always about creativity. Sometimes it is about simply putting in the time, walking the miles, continuing the fight. Sometimes putting in the time is probably the most important part of success.

I believe this is true; that you have to kill the Buddha when you see him on the road, because the Buddha is really within you and the illusion of his presence can be a delusion. Still, sometimes I can't even seem to *find* the Buddha inside myself!

I am not myself when I am away from the "work," in spite of appearances. Perhaps I look the same to my friends, to my husband, but I know better. I am suffering from a malaise that tells me I will never write anything again. It is a terrible, deep, frightening feeling. I feel lazy and useless. All my accomplishments mean nothing. I am in the doldrums. I can't catch the dreams, let alone the inspiring winds of creativity.

And, like the old battlefield, there is blood and bone in the grass, and when the wind and weather stream over the remains of the battle, the rain soaks the places where dreams have died, the weather and time prepares the ground for the new, the flowers and the birds and their songs that will follow in the spring. But when will the spring come? It drags by this year, threatening to turn into summer before anything begins, before I can write one new song, or work on one new chapter.

I go back to my forms, the true north needle of where I am and where I want to go. I think about my process and make a list of what I know and what will help me:

- Just start. Even if what you're doing is bad. No action is lost; the results will show up in some other place, not always in the place where you put the work.

- Let your judgment go.
- Do what you love, talk about what you know.
- Write about where you want to go and what you want to do.
- Believe that you will find what you are looking for.
- Listen to music that inspires you.
- Read books that will inspire you to write, to think about things differently.
- Write all the time; nothing is junk, don't throw it out the first day, it may reveal something to you later.
- Keep notebooks, jot down quotes from the books you read; keep writing and reading as part of your daily life.

On a pad of paper by my bed, I have a list on a small blue piece of paper. This morning I look at it, and promise myself I will do the things on the list I have written before going to sleep.

- Wake
- Write dreams
- Meditate
- Write in journal
- Write songs
- Practice piano
- Learn songs
- Exercise

Each item on this list is like a linchpin that helps me get up the mountain, a foothold that moves me forward, a habit pattern that has been set but must be polished and practiced each day. And having the list helps me to actually do most everything.

I read the meditation books beside the bed. I have my coffee. The first thing I think of, after I write in my journal, after I try to catch my dreams before they float away in the morning light, is music and words, songs and lyrics. How do I make this day say something to me that is beautiful, fresh, and different? To make a day that is beautiful, I put something in my room that will make me feel like smiling—a painting, a stained-glass lamp, a new plant.

The years of practicing the piano taught me that my fingers must be ready for the big concerto, as well as for the day's exercises. It helped me begin discipling myself to work creatively early on in my life. The discipline of my creative life helps me to change my habits for the better. I try to do this in every way possible. I also discipline myself to be rested and positive, to exercise and eat well, to let the soap opera go, to find ways to be open to the experience of creativity anywhere it finds me, or I find it.

The material often dictates the form of the discipline. If I am writing a song, I must sit in one place, usually at the piano, working and reworking the lyric and the melody, with a tape recorder at my elbow, and paper to write on, until I have wrestled the shape of the song into something that will last—perhaps only until tomorrow, but that is something to hold on to.

Or to let go of.

But if I am working on a book my discipline will take a different shape.

I was taught by my parents that creativity is about making a life—making music, sewing clothes, making meals, writing songs, making our Christmas card every year—writing the poem, putting the glue on the paper and the shiny tinsel, sending our holiday missive out into the world, to friends and relatives, letting the world know that we were thinking of them, and that we loved them.

Love was being creative about who you were, who you could become. If you loved others, you would love yourself, help yourself to become all that you could become.

That meant studying and learning, which were all part of the creative process. You learned to read, and then to count and to draw. I had my lessons at school, and my lessons on the piano. And I loved learning.

My singing has brought me a career of international proportions that has taught me discipline. I have to keep my body fit, I have to keep my attitude positive, I have to eat and sleep and walk and talk in a healthy manner. I cannot afford the luxury of whining, and I cannot afford the sloth of letting my body or my mind go, for then they would not be ready for the long tour, the short walk, the days on end on airplanes and cars, the hotel rooms and the stages on which I make my living.

And if I am not disciplined about my writing, I will not get any writing done! Nor any songs written.

There is talent, and there is the discipline to get the talent to pay out. I have to harness the talent, use the discipline, and I then find that, surprise, there is pleasure in the discipline, and the discipline will say to me, I am not your enemy! I am your friend!

Finally, the malaise lifts, and I can see clearly again. But these times are not ever entirely over, and I must always be willing to go back to discipline for the lessons it brings of freedom.

Discipline is freedom, disguised as a cell. It holds its own secret. The cell is its own door, and discipline is the key.

Chapter 4

Remembering

Creativity is a voice that calls us from dreams, that peeks out of the corner of our eyes when we think no one is looking, the longing that breaks our hearts even when we think we should be happiest, and to which we cannot give a name. When I was young, I heard the voice, the ticking, had the dream, but I didn't know what it was and only felt the pain, the longing that the voice inside brought me.

—Judy Collins, *Voices*, 1994

emory is often the ground in which we toil to make beauty, and must be refreshed and revitalized by looking and listening to the stories and the pictures in our minds. Some of them are painful, and some are sweet. It is in this mixture, sweet and unbearable, that we find the recipe for the beauty that we are seeking.

In writing and singing about memories, I often feel I have to crack through a wall of tears. The tears are often part of the barrier that keeps me from my creativity. But remembering can bring pleasure as well as pain. If I am singing a song that brings me to tears, I have to cry those tears before I can be fully present in singing that song. No one wants to hear a blubbering singer, or read a blubbering writer! Breaking through the barrier and getting my feelings out in private makes the creation or performance easier and more pleasurable for me. And, especially in the case of a performance, it may make the experience more poignant for whoever is listening and watching, so that someone else can cry, someone else can feel what I do.

But I must do my sobbing on my own, not in public.

In order to survive remembering, I try to include in each day the things that sustain, that amuse, that nurture me, for all of these things are creative. They are the ground from which I rise when I imagine; they are the soil in which I find the seeds for new growth, new poetry. I would like to think I am in a remembering, creative state all the time, but usually the muse has her own schedule, and the phrases and the inspiration come when I am sitting at the computer, or at the piano, and not at the dentist. Although these places can feel like the dentist when nothing is coming!

I remember a photo of me at my grandmother's house in

Seattle when I had learned to walk at nine months. I am on tip-toe, reaching up to put my fingers on the keys of the piano. I remember, too, the bluebirds in their nest outside the window, and my standing with my ear on the window, listening to their songs.

I remember snow in Seattle one winter when I was still very little. My mother had to put a leash on me to keep me from running "every which way." I settled down only to play the piano for a half hour, then an hour, then two at a stretch. It was the only thing that calmed down my frantic search to see everything, talk to everyone, and know everything.

So the words and the music, and the books that were read to me, and that I learned to read so early, before I was four, were my refuge, my salvation. Music was the entrance into who I was, who I am.

Who I will become.

The discipline of practicing the piano was one of the first stones in the metaphorical house I was building. The house that would become the place I would thrive and grow as a musician. And so, music and books molded me, made me what I am.

My teachers played a great part in forming my creative life. Most of them were bright, gifted people who loved what they did and imparted a love of knowledge to me. They made me yearn to create something that would serve to help me find meaning in my life, as well as inspire others. So both in word and music I had my beginnings, and in words and music I continue to live my life.

Mrs. Munch taught me in the first and second grades. She had a beehive in her window, where the bees scurried and hurried through the little caves and tunnels and we could see them work, and she would say, "You see, they are always busy."

I didn't have to learn from the bees about busy. I was born busy.

I walked to school past the Lark Ellen School for boys—for lost boys, my mother said. One of them kissed me during the hayride on Halloween in 1947, my first kiss. I bought double bubble Bazooka chewing gum and some girls tickled me till I fell down on the school playground, giggling and laughing till I thought I would die. Those moments of trying to be in the in group, letting them take me for all I was worth, would teach me lessons later on, when I would swear I wouldn't let myself be sucked into whatever it was that passed for group membership. I became more of a loner, till I was in junior high school, where I met my friends Carol and Marcia. Art bound us together.

Carol and Marcia were both dancers, and we didn't have to fall down screaming with laughter while one tormented the other. We could make art, and became the Little Reds—performing *Little Red Riding Hood,* they dancing the parts while I played the piano. I found my membership in the most important group there was to me—the creative group. I began to shine in the school shows and in the concerts I did for my piano teacher's students, and for my father's radio show.

By that time, my brother David was one and Michael was

three and I was seven. We lived in West Los Angeles. It was a house of activity and constant motion, with Mother and Daddy, and the three of us children. Fluffy would sleep on my bed. One morning I awoke and found she had had kittens, five little balls of fur, wet and tiny, but I didn't know what was happening, so I leaped out of bed and told my mother that Fluffy had fallen apart.

I have often found that things must fall apart
before they can come together.

This house on the lake that I share with my partner, lover, and husband, Louis Nelson, has been the scene of many creative ideas and projects over the last twenty-six years we have been together. Usually we go up to the house when I don't have to be on the road giving concerts, or recording or doing other projects in the city.

I love puttering and cooking, moving between the stove and the piano, the computer and the chopping board. Garlic and onions simmering in oil accompany Guy Noir and Lake Wobegon on those treasured Saturday nights, and Garrison Keillor's voice floating across the big open space of the downstairs living room as I putter and chop, peel and toss.

I have written some of what I think are my best songs here, including "The Blizzard," which I pounded out in a night and a

morning in 1988 when I was finishing the preparations for a
show in Aspen with Kris Kristofferson. Watching the snow fall
outside the windows of the Ridgefield house a few days before
the planned trip to Aspen, I became suffused with a pain about
the fact that I didn't have a song about Colorado. When we
moved to Colorado from Los Angeles in 1949, my father
quickly wrote a song about Colorado.

He had written a song about the state that we all love so pas-
sionately, even those of us who had moved to other places made
our way back at least once a year to ski, or in the summer to
hike. But I did not have a song! That ate away at me as I practiced downstairs, looking out at this willow tree and trying to
think what I could do about it.

It was early December and the show was planned for Christmas. I sat down in the afternoon, watching the snow fall outside, from late afternoon to late at night. By the morning the
song was fundamentally done.

Colorado, Colorado
When the world leaves you shivering
And the blizzard blows
When the snow flies and the night falls
There's a light in the window and a place called home
At the end of the storm
One night on the mountain I was headed for Estes
When the roads turned to ice and it started to snow

Put on the chains in a whirl of white powder
Halfway up to Berthoud near a diner I know
And the light burned inside, shining down through
  the snowfall
God it was cold and the temperature droppin'
Went in for coffee and shivered as I drank it
Warm in my hands in the steam as it rose

Sitting there at the counter was a dark-headed stranger
Me and the owner and him keepin' warm
Nodded hello and I said it's a cold one
Looks like there might be a blizzard tonight—
And "Yes," said the owner, "there's a big storm on the mountain
Good thing we're open, we could be here for hours
There's nothing for miles and it's too late to get to Denver
Better not try for the summit tonight"

And the snow fell
And the night passed
And I talked to the strangers
While the blizzard blew

Me and the stranger, you know I don't talk to strangers
I'm a private sort of person but a blizzard is a blizzard
And somehow I found myself saying you'd left me
Tellin' him everything I wanted to say to you

You know how it is when you can talk to a stranger
Someone you're quite sure you'll never see again—
Soon we were laughin', and talkin', and drinkin'
He said, "You must know you're too good for him"

And the snow fell
And the night passed
And I talked to the stranger
While the blizzard blew

The stranger said, "Love it can cry you a river—
Me, I'm a loner 'cause I can't take the heartache
And sometimes I'm a fighter when I get too much whiskey—
Here have a little whiskey, pretend you don't give a damn—
My cabin's up here on the side of the mountain
You can go up there and sleep through the blizzard"
I put on my parka, said good-bye to the owner
Followed the stranger through the snow up the mountainside

Woke in the morning to the sun on the snow
My car was buried in six feet of snowdrifts
They dug me out, just the owner and the stranger
Sent me on my way when the snowplow had been by

And the roads were all clear and the sun on the mountains
Sparkled like diamonds on the peak to peak highway

Then I knew that I would get over you, knew you could leave me
But you'd never break me

Colorado, Colorado
When the world leaves you shivering
And the blizzard blows
When the snow flies and the night falls
There's a light in the window and a place called home
At the end of the storm

Colorado, Colorado
When the world leaves you shivering
And the blizzard blows
When the snow flies and the night falls
There's a light in the window and a place called home
At the end of the storm

I could see in the song the face of the stranger, a man I had
known many years before in Colorado, a friend, a pal, a sometime lover. I saw the snow, the pine trees that hold snow in their
arms in the big blizzards. I saw my life, deeply rooted as it is in
the mind, in memory, in song, in the phrases of lyrics I sing and
in the spaces I travel in and the beauty of the world around me.
I was no longer in a whiskey blur, and I knew that the song was
really not about an old lover or an old memory of love at all,
but about the passion of my heart for Colorado and about the

struggle to leave the whiskey behind. Without having left it behind, I would never be writing.

And so, remembering brought the song to life.

Memory is always with us. There are times when I think I
live mostly in my mind, and the memories of beauty, strange
and powerful, pull me into the places I need to go. I polish, I
rearrange, like the maker of a puzzle, inspired by whatever
muse is watching over me, and by the great puzzle maker Himself. My memory serves me and I serve my Maker, to do and
be what He needs and wants.

Memory resonates all through our days.

Chapter 5

Reading

Whoever you are, your true place is calling, and because you are a spark of the Divine, you will never be content until you answer.

—Emmet Fox, *Around the Year*, 1991

Since I was a very young child, reading has been my friend and my consolation and a great part of my education. The books of friends, the guidance of good book reviews, the books I read in school, and the rumors of what good book is out there that I might find interesting. I am guided by my instincts, now, as I was by my teachers and my father and mother in the beginning. To fill a rainy afternoon with a book and a cup of coffee is, to me, heaven on earth. And I feel my reading is part of the creative process. It helps me to learn a little every day.

A library is a sacred place, as are the bookshelves that fill my home. Reading is also part of my formula for work. And when I think about the books I have not read and that wait for me, I am off in a cloud of desire and wonder—there is so much to read!

I would go to the library in West Los Angeles when I was six and seven to listen to the librarian read to us. I don't even remember the stories, but they are here in my mind somewhere, repeating themselves to me. "Everything is going to come out just fine." Or maybe not. But there is a lesson in that, too. I can feel almost a chill of waiting for the mystery to be solved, for the lovers to reconcile, for the end to be reached. Going through all it takes to get to the end. Or the beginning.

You could say that, even amid my travels and singing engagements, my book writing and songwriting, and the myriad other things I do in life, perhaps my favorite avocation is reading. I read as widely and as voraciously as I did when I was growing up. My hunger has not faltered for what lies ahead and my reading ranges from history to biography to mystery and other fiction as well. Antonia Fraser, Ron Chernow, David McCullough, Churchill; Madeleine Albright, President Grant; P. D. James, Wilkie Collins, Pat Conroy, Peter Matheson.

Actually, my first level of consciousness—the subterranean

level, so to speak—is the voice; the words, the melody of speech. The first sound we hear. You are who words make you, at first. Information. About what to eat, and when. About what is right to do, and what you should not ever, ever do. You will make money if you are good and lucky and work hard. You will not do well if you tell lies. The words of my parents, of my friends, of my teachers. So sound was my first teacher, and language. Printed words. I read music before I could read print, but the print followed quickly, and I became a voracious reader even when five and six years old.

I often write and think about my family, my mother and father, my brothers and sister. Though my father is gone, he is still very much a part of my psyche and my imagination. He was inventive and very funny and always saw (though he could not see, you remember!) the bright side of things, the other side of the question, the glass totally full. Brothers, each with gifts and talents, and my sister, so creative and artistic and such an amazing mother, are so beloved, and I think of them and, sometimes, write songs about them.

My mother, Marjorie, when we were young, made all our clothes, turning out calico shirts for the boys and skirts for me, on the Singer sewing machine with its foot treadle humming in her bedroom, which served as sewing and sleeping room. She got the patterns from Simplicity, and spread out the tissue paper on the fabric on the floor in the living room. She and I would often shop for material, as I grew older, and choose the plain or patterned fabric, and I would follow my mother's example, running my fingers over cotton and silk, corduroy and velvet. I loved the process of watching her make clothes that grew from thin air and imagination into our clothing, fine and well-made.

But always no matter what was happening in our family, we were read to, or reading. Books were part of the fabric, the food, the drink, the nourishment of the family myth, and the family growth.

I read many books about spirituality and creativity, because they help me focus on letting go and letting the inner voices guide me to where I am supposed to go. The first step for me is to have the attitude that eliminates negativity. For some writers and creative people, negativity may be a driving force, a hammer on the nail, something that they can use to further their work. *I have found negativity does not work for me, and so every day of my life I work to get it out of the way.*

This does not mean that I do not write and sing about difficult, painful things. Life is painful and full of pitfalls, and like everyone, I have had terrible things happen to me. Being positive does not make me exempt from the trials. But the negative energy, if I let it, will also bring me down and, I know, possibly kill me. I finally believe one can be positive even in the most terrifying situations.

My sister, Holly, observing this quality over our fifty-one years of siblinghood, often tells me that I am simply deluded, and ought to wake up and smell the trouble that exists in the world. I tell her I am quite aware of it, but I am not ever, if I have anything to say about it, going to succumb to it in my emotional and inner life. But then, Holly often lets her own optimism shine! Within, hope *always* prevails. There, the light always shines. Thus my creative job is to let that light from within shine from without as well.

I never feel compelled to finish a book I do not like, or feel is not well-written. Biographies, such as the book I am reading at the present, the riveting life of Alexander Hamilton by Ron Chernow, can overtake me as though I were reading a novel and I run to read it at every free moment.

I feel the excitement in my stomach when I come upon a new writer with promise, or one of the old standbys like Graham Greene or Yeats or Melville or Conan Doyle.

I find in a journal from last year a list of all the books I was reading:

Paris 1919, Margaret MacMillan, foreword by Richard
  Holbrooke
The Diary of Alice James
Marie Antoinette, Antonia Fraser
Elizabeth I, CEO, Alan Axelrod
E = mc², A Biography of the World's Most Famous Equation,
  David Bodanis

Master of the Senate, Robert Caro

The Bridge, Gay Talese

My Name Is Bill, Susan Cheever

Castles of Steel, Robert Massie

The Murder Room, P. D. James

Appointment in Samarra, John O'Hara

Sea of Glory, Nathaniel Philbrick

The Other House, Henry James

Age of Jackson, Arthur M. Schlesinger, Jr.

The Great Fire, Shirley Hazzard

Elizabeth and Mary, Jane Dunn

The House by the Sea, May Sarton—again!

Emerson: The Mind on Fire, Robert Richardson, Jr.

The Devil in the White City, Erik Larson

Salt, Mark Kurlansky

The Intimate Merton, Thomas Merton

The Unknown Night: The Genius and Madness of R.A. Blakelock,
    Glyn Vincent

Nine Horses, Billy Collins

Around the Year with Emmet Fox, Emmet Fox

All of Harry Potter

Mary, Queen of Scots and the Murder of Lord Darnley, Alison Weir

The Volcano Lover, Susan Sontag

Becoming Light, Erica Jong

But Melville will always hold a special place in my heart.
Probably the first book I really knew in the gut was *Moby-*

Dick, which was read to my siblings and me by our Melville-obsessed father, who read things in Braille, from huge volumes that came in the mail from the Library of Congress every couple of weeks. A copy of *Moby-Dick* in Braille took up three feet in the big bookshelf, or stood in the corner as high as my chest.

A passage of Ishmael's monologue still stays with me, a meditation on life and death and whaling and the soul. . . . "Yes, there is death in this business of whaling—a speechlessly quick, chaotic bundling of a man into eternity. But what then? Methinks we have hugely mistaken this matter of Life and Death. Methinks that what they call my shadow here on earth is my true substance. . . . Methinks my body is but the lees of my better self. In fact take my body who will take it, I say, it's not me. And therefore three cheers for Nantucket; and come a stove boat and stove body when they will, for stove my soul, Jove himself cannot!!" (Penguin Classics, page 42.)

Stove my soul, Jove himself cannot!

From *Moby-Dick* much of my own philosophy of life came, and from the Methodists with their plain hymnal and polished wood and white-painted walls and simplicity. From *Moby-Dick,* the Brontë sisters, Dostoyevsky and Tolstoy, Albert Camus. I read *L'Étranger* in French in high school, absorbing the strange, exotic feel of Algeria and the desert, and the voice of aloneness in what I knew was a different way of thinking, the French way, rather than my small town, Denver, Colorado, way.

I would learn that there was much in that Denver upbringing that would give me solace and solidity, vision and hope, in all the years to come.

But first I would have to move from Denver to New York to find that my yearnings always lead me back to the West.

Every time I pick up a new book, whether a history of the West or a biography of a politician or a mystery that thrills me; each time I find a new writer who intrigues and delights, I am expanding the joy of my reading, and know that as long as I live, there will be new authors, and new books to find that take me on the journeys I need to experience. Like the cave drawings, the books of early and ancient history; whether the Bible or the Koran, the Torah or the latest translation of the *Bhagavad Gita* by Stephen Levine,

I yearn for books to teach and entertain, to challenge and enlighten and educate me.

Reading is always part of my life, and I believe my reading contributes to the creative process no matter what we may be creating.

Today I am in Seattle, in the middle of my Christmas tour. I am singing Christmas songs and have a choir each night, so that I hear the music even more sweetly from children's and teenagers' choirs, and the occasional adult choir. On the planes and in the cars as I travel through the countryside, I have my books. On this trip I am finishing the Joseph Ellis book on Washington, learning about parallel lives after having read Ron Chernow's book on Alexander Hamilton, seeing where these amazing men's lives crossed, understanding more about how this country with its preposterous, delirious dream came to be—through one hard and brilliant day's actions after another, as well as through a kind of synchronicity that still defies rationality.

Also, I just finished a very good mystery thriller that my sister Holly recommended. We both like to read P. D. James and Elizabeth George, so I am thrilled to find another Brit, Peter Robinson, and have just finished his thriller *Playing with Fire*.

I am learning, and also getting a great thrill from all kinds of books. Reading gives joy and education and lights up new places and new ideas. Reading is perhaps my first real vocation!

Chapter 6

Time

You have all the time in the world.
Time is on my side.
Tempus fugit.
Time waits for no man.
Time on my hands.
Time stands still.

—Traditional sayings

ime often seems to expand when I am working on a project, depending on my mood, or the weather, or the things I am thinking about. You might find that if you are immersed in the creative process, time can seem to shift. The time you have, and work with, can expand or diminish, depending on the lightness of your being, or the heaviness of your mood. Time is a place of wonder, and of shifting value.

In the study of space and the universe that is called string theory, all time is happening all the time, and all events, past, present, and future, are happening simultaneously. Perhaps that may explain the nature of expanding and contracting time in our lives. In string theory, there are wormholes, in which one can travel to any time that has happened in the past, or in the future.

Perhaps, if we believe in string theory, we really do have all the time in the world, forever.

The questions of time and the uncontrollable things in life become almost questions of magic, for time can open up, or close down, depending on your inner feeling for time. And the illusive can be captured, for a moment, but not for long.

> *It slips away, while we are wondering*
> *how much of it we have.*
> *It appears, when we think we have*
> *not got enough of it.*
> *It opens to accommodate our needs*
> *when we least expect it to.*

I get an idea for a book or for a song, and begin to think first about the creative process. I want to write some songs in the coming months, how am I going to do that when there are also other pressing things I must do? I hope not to resort to the solution I used when I was fourteen and trying to learn a difficult piece of music. I took a bottle of pills because I didn't think I had enough time to make the performance perfect.

Now I have a little trick that I use to fool time, and at times it works!

I decide to write a song a day for thirty days. I get my notebook set (I always need new notebooks for exercises like this—something about that clean paper in September when school is starting!), and then I start, adhering to my prom not to judge, but to just put down a song a day. It may take me five minutes; it may take me twenty minutes. I give myself a time limit; I am not going to spend more than, say, half an hour at the most. The subject can be anything. It can start with a phrase I have heard, like, "After you've seen the truth, the rest is just cheap whiskey." I write for a month, every day, and I write by hand. Of course, others will say they have to write prose by hand, as well—my friend Erica Jong writes everything by hand, on yellow pads, and then dictates or has someone copy her work. Whatever works for you.

Then, when a month, or ninety days, or whatever the allotted time I have given myself to do this exercise, is over, I must write all these handwritten songs into a notebook so they are clear and legible. I will make changes to them that will fill them out, bringing them closer to being actual songs.

This is an exercise to get the creativity moving, and I may abandon it midstream, as the juices are flowing on their own and the starter motor of an exercise is no longer needed. But when I am copying down the thirty or the ninety songs in ninety days, I find a lot of things that surprise me. I write about things that I didn't know I was interested in, that I never thought I would have the time to think about.

It is important for me to write poems and songs by hand. I write prose with a typewriter (a computer) but I must write the things that have a flow of phrasing and an immediacy by hand.

For the creative process, the problem that must be solved is that of time. Before I was forty, I didn't see how I could achieve that kind of seamless connection to my creative work that my friend Susan Cheever showed me is possible. The gradual assumption of a working process has been slow but steady. It meant giving up a great deal of my neurotic preoccupation with perfection, and knowing that to sing, to eat, to breathe, to write a song, to work on a book, could all be part of a flow of connection to whoever my muse, my angel speaking from the Gods and Goddesses, might be. I had to be open to alternatives for creativity, since my traveling life means I have to find time on the road to stay connected to the work, and not think that the only way I was going to achieve anything was to somehow get a year off to start that novel I always intended to write. I had to accept that the novel, if I did it a day at a time and went on with the rest of my life, would get written only if I sat down and wrote for an hour or so, every day.

The lessons we learn come with time, but art is not usually learned on a specific timetable. Of course, there are milestones to learning and perhaps they happen at average ages. In our early teens we most likely have a glimpse of who we are starting out to be; in our mid-twenties we have learned a lot but probably think we know more than we do; around forty maybe we wish we could go back to school and probably realize that we are going to have to teach ourselves, or gather the lessons on our own, as we go; in our sixties we understand that we don't know much but have a few ground rules and can't wait to see what is around the next bend.

But the time is ripe at every age, and time bends with the horizon and takes on the color and the feel of dawn almost any day.

Success is not about time. In fact, some people are incredibly successful at things they don't even start until much later in life.

- How to plan my time?
- When will I find the time?
- How can I fill the time?
- Is there ever going to be time?
- I have too much time!
- How can I wait that long?
- How will I get this done in time?
- Where has the time gone?

These are the questions that come up again and again when I am thinking about the creative process. I am in the middle of making a new record. When will I find time to do the writing on the liner notes? How will I get my practicing done so that when I have to perform the songs, I will know them well enough to feel comfortable?

Mostly, I surrender to the fact
that the time is now!

Noon

ime for a delicious meal, a whole-grain sandwich, a glass of sparkling water, maybe some steamed vegetables. I might even have lunch with a friend, if I feel I am far enough ahead on my work. Wondrous conversation, nurturing food! A book for an hour, maybe a nap! And a lesson, or a trip to the museum.

I break my morning work and get on with whatever the day

may bring. There are meetings to attend, for my business and when I am at the end of a project, mixing sessions for a CD, or review sessions with my editor or publisher. The day is full of promise, for I have done the work I intended to do, and so I can go off to rewrite, or lunch, or meetings, with a light heart. I can get on the Internet and do finances, meeting with my office people, with agents and project managers.

And there might be physical or talk therapy! It is my conviction that we need all the help we can get, and if therapy helps, as it has helped me over the years, I do whatever it is to break the isolation and to get the encouragement I need.

Chapter 7

Observing

What does the sand look like?

y eyes are not the only way I look. I feel, I sense, I know inside something that may not be visible.

Just keeping awake to what is around you is a good exercise.

Try observing the way people talk. Listen to phrases. Look at colors. If you are a painter, get a notebook and pull it out to sketch what you see, write your memory of the way someone in a movie said, "When you've heard the truth, the rest is just cheap whiskey." Write a song about that. A cartoon. Do a little drawing that uses that in the text, above the figure, in a little balloon.

Songs, and cartoons, are sometimes just different comments on the world.

Observe the way people stand when they are resting after an exhausting run in Central Park; when they have entered a room and not yet been asked to take a seat; when they are waiting for a train.

Put your observations in your little book and then transfer them to your notebook for use later this day, or this week, or this life. Sometimes I find a phrase that I wrote when I was twenty-three. I will use it somewhere.

Nothing is ever lost.

Observe that an object or subject changes by the act of observation. A scientist said recently that when a thing is learned, one's biology changes. I believe I understand what that means, and I believe that I have changed physically at times when I have learned something.

I try to be aware, to listen, to read the paper, listen to NPR or watch the news on television. I have to admit I am fond of reading *The New Yorker* and *The Nation* and *Vanity Fair*, as opposed to a trashy novel, but I do delve into the trash, from time to time, watch a bad movie, pick up a copy of *Exposé* magazine. Contrast is everything.

I try to keep up with the new books that I want to read, with the politics of the day, no matter how angry or exultant that might make me. I notice what people wear, what they say. I try to carry a notebook with me to write down the things that I observe during the day, phrases I hear that take my breath away, or make me smile, or float lyrically by, or arrest me by their harsh and sudden violence.

Sometimes I try looking at something, then looking away and describing what was left in my mind, what the colors or the trees were, the scent on the wind, whether a bird flew by, what the makes of the cars were in a street scene. Of course, nowadays, the cars look so much alike unless they are ten years old that it is hard to know! I try to observe what the weather is like, and if the sun was on my face.

Sometimes I do a crossword—to stretch my mind.

My father was blind, but he went everywhere without a Seeing Eye dog and never used a cane, except in later years when he was made the head of an organization for the blind in Denver. There, the head of the organization told Daddy he simply *had* to use a cane, that to have a blind man in a position of responsibility who did not use a cane would make others feel bad.

I think part of the reason I was so eager to create, and be and do something was so that my father would see me. And sometimes, I thought that it wasn't that he was blind, but that I was invisible.

⚜

I knew Daddy trained himself to "see," when he was a little boy. There were stories he told us of his bizarre adventures in the special school he went to, taking the "deaf" children skating because everyone forgot Charlie didn't know how to see, but somehow he got the kids there and back without mishap. He wore blue glass eyes and if you didn't know he was blind, you wouldn't, at least for a while. His demeanor was one of complete attention at all times. I think his secret was being totally and absolutely attuned to everything around him.

He often told the story of the little dog that laughed. A tiny old terrier used to sit in the room with Daddy when others were gone, and try not to make any noise, so that Daddy wouldn't hear him and throw him out of the room at the School for the Blind in Gooding, Idaho. As the two, man and dog, sat in the room, Daddy's hands probably running over a Braille book, or musing quietly, the dog would not be able to withhold his voice, and would begin to laugh, giving himself away.

It was as though a phantom passed through the room when my father saw and heard things that were not there. The ghosts from the past in Idaho and on the Snake River, the frat brothers putting him behind the wheel of a Model T and driving it around the campus. It was a testament to Daddy's illusion of sight that the guys who witnessed the driving blind man, at least for a moment, believed it was totally possible. His persona was that convincing.

As I grew up I tried many things to see if I could figure out how he saw so well.

We lived in a home where the visual was not as present, because of my father's blindness. I feel I have only learned to "see" in these later years since his death.

I go off to a museum to absorb art and the experience of the day by myself. It is an important ingredient to finding out what I think and what I see, what I remember, on my own, without the influence of another. I walk from time to time, I stroll on the avenues of the great city I live in. I look at people and think about nothing in particular, or perhaps in depth about my life and about my work. I love to shop alone, perhaps out of guilty pleasure!

Even where there is no reason, the desire to write and to create, to write a song, paint a painting, write a poem or a story, will drive us to work. We write to tell stories; we write to find out what the sand looks like.

In *The New York Times* the other day was an article about the National Endowment for the Arts programs in military bases—Fort Bragg, North Carolina; Fort Hood, Texas; Fort Reilly, Kansas—where professional writers are brought in to teach the soldiers about writing. The teachers asked these young men and women in their sessions to keep journals and to write about what they saw. One of the questions was "What does sand look like?" They are, many of them, going to go to Iraq. It would be a good idea to know what sand looks like, and what Muslims think about and what they study and what their lives are like.

I thrilled to think of literate soldiers and the ad for the Military NEA program—

> *We will teach you how to win wars with words!*
> —The U.S. Army

The bottom line they are given is the same for all of us who aspire to do something creatively—to do it, write it, draw it every day and be as detailed as possible.

All around me there is evidence of things great and beautiful, if I will but open my eyes and my heart. If I take a walk in a museum or go to a garden for an afternoon during my week, I will find myself delighted by something unexpected, taken down a path I never dreamed of going.

I see someone, they say something, I catch a phrase, think of a song, imagine a new watercolor. I want to paint with silver and gold, I think, passing by an illuminated painting of the Virgin in the Metropolitan. I have thoughts that want to come out in a song that could be a movie, I think while I am watching a movie, seeing a play; there are songs here that will draw me in and never let me down, I think as I hear the opera.

I was listening to Billie Holiday sing the other day when I was at the dentist. He was pulling a tooth and playing Billie! I asked him if he had ever heard her sing. He said he was too young for that, chuckling (it was easy for him to do, he had both hands in my mouth!); but he said he did know something about her, and that was that she had died with seventy-five dollars in her stocking and a needle in her arm.

What an image for a song, and I am working on one now, having found the right phrase at the dentist, while having a tooth pulled.

All things are fuel for the creative mind when it is at work.

○

Yesterday there were swans on the lake in Ridgefield, where my husband, Louis, and I have a house. The birds were clambering to get at a downed willow branch that had broken off during a recent storm and fallen, full of summer leaves, into the lake in front of our house. The swans ducked their heads in and out of the water, amid the green leaves of the willow, salvaging what they could of the rare leaves. Both white, long-necked parents bent to the task, their feathered necks bobbing up and down in the sparkling water under the tree. Four cygnets, teenagers according to swan years, three gray and one white, with no sleek feathers as yet, eventually became bored at their parents' preoccupation and left, wandering off to another part of the lake, leaving their parents to duck for willow leaves until the mother, raising her head, reluctantly left the job of willow retrieval and swam off to her bored teenagers, leaving her mate to continue bobbing in the bright water.

I supposed that, not being able to reach the willow leaves even on the best days with their long swan necks, this rare treat held their attention as if it had been a tray of sweets in front of a sugar addict.

All birds fascinate me, because they can fly and most of them can sing. I always knew that I had to sing in order to fly.

I have my favorite birds. Some are mellifluous and liquid, cheery and heartbreaking at the same time. Thoreau says about one of the birds of the Northeast, perhaps the purple finch, one of my favorites:

> *Whenever a man hears it he is young and Nature is in her spring; wherever he hears it, it is a new world and a free country, and the gates of heaven are not shut against him . . .*

I remember dreaming one night when I was a child of a tree filled with birds of all the colors of the rainbow. The birds sang, and then they flew, taking to the sky with their wings. I watch for their flights, listen for their songs in nature as well as when I am watching a British mystery! I remember their power in my childhood, and when I see a sparrow on the ground in New York, I often stop to watch him, hopping, pecking at seeds or bagel crumbs, flying away up to a nest in a tree in the park or the hollow metal funnel of a stoplight, and I think, there, little singer, I know your flight and your struggle, I am like you, singing and working, singing and working.

Piaf was called the little sparrow, and the president I know the best so far, William Jefferson Clinton, was referred to during his administration as Eagle One. When I was ten I was given a parakeet and his songs and his spirit I will never forget. I taught him to talk, to say things like "Birds can't talk," and he called out my name when I came home from school, flying to land on my head, "Hi, Judy!" He would sing in his bright voice. He sat on our shoulders at dinner and ate from our mouths, a habit that some friends found disgusting! And when one day, when his wings weren't clipped short enough, he flew off into a February landscape in Denver, I wept for weeks and don't think I have ever really gotten over his absence in my life. How strange, it may seem to some, to be so attached to a bird, a tiny thing with wings, a spirit of such seeming insignificance. Not to me.

When I was nineteen and pregnant with my son, Clark, my husband and I hiked into Rocky Mountain National Park and on the side of the trail just before the water flowing down from the snowmelt, in among the pine trees and Douglas fir, I saw a hummingbird with a bright orange body, hovering at ten thousand feet above sea level. People said he couldn't have been there, it was too high for such a vividly colored South American creature, but he was there, and I saw him and I remember him to this day, daring little fellow, up there with the columbines, and the fourteen-thousand-foot peaks of Colorado. What tales he would tell back in Guatemala, or wherever he returned to.

I often put birds in my songs, singing birds, birds of prey, who are creatures of the wind and the imagination, too—and birds that flock and birds that talk and birds that hum and birds that promise spring, singing in their lilting, enchanting voices.

Sometimes I doubt I could sing if there were no birds to teach me memory and beauty, singing through the seasons, singing for themselves, and for us.

And then the swans! Seeing them is the kind of experience that always triggers the ideas of self-expression for me. I think of paintings, of songs, and of stories. I later learned that the willow tree is the source of aspirin. No wonder those swans were so happy!

○

The observations we make in our daily lives can add to the creativity we are pursuing. The things we look at, really look at, and resolve to remember, are important. Get an ear for the common speech, an eye for the beauty in the world.

*Observations contribute to our sense of wonder
and feed our dreams and our hearts.*

Learning

*L*earning new things and facing new challenges has always been an important and thrilling part of my life. They say playing chess helps one to learn about other things. I learned chess when I was young and married to my first husband. We played until I beat him, and never played again!

I have recently begun to play again, and know the process makes me happy and challenges me. I started doing crossword puzzles for the same reason. I like to find new things that push my mind, and hone my intellect. Keeping my mind sharp helps me in all areas of my life.

You may want to take a class in a discipline different from, but related to, what you do professionally—say, a watercolor class if you are used to painting in oil; a tap dance class if you are a dancer of ballet; a film class if you are a singer.

Sometimes I have found the stimulation of another discipline helps to make my primary creativity even richer.

If you truly want something rich and nurturing in your life, you can find ways to get there.

I wanted to tell the story of my great piano teacher, Dr. Brico, and so I found people who could work with me and help me make a movie about her life, and although I don't make my living as a filmmaker today, the process taught me a great deal about phrasing in film editing, that it was similar to music, and about telling a story. This has actually helped my songwriting and taught me a new way to get an idea across to an audience.

The main thing is to never listen when people tell you that you can't do something simply because it is not what you do, or have done. I find that often it is just such a time when venturing to learn something new is most important.

The light is slanted across the Hudson River and I take a jacket and head out into the day, for a lesson—a singing lesson. I did this for thirty-two years in New York, going to stand in front of the harp or the piano to listen to the voice of my singing teacher, Max Margulies, tell me about Yvette Guilbert and Adelina Patti, and Ghelli—all the great singers of the early part of the twentieth century. We would listen to them, and then listen to Frank Sinatra and Ella Fitzgerald, singers Max felt were equal to the greatest of the greats in singing technique. Over tea, in front of his de Kooning and Gorky paintings, the light would fade and wander, as the notes I sang meandered in the afternoon light. Standing in front of a man of genius, I spent the hours, and learned how to sing.

Max knew de Kooning well. When they were young and lived in the East Village, after de Kooning had arrived in New York as a stowaway on a ship, they even shared a winter coat in their early poor years. Gorky and de Kooning both paid their bills with paintings, and gave paintings as presents to Max, who made his living by playing the violin and writing music criticism and giving voice lessons, about which he had learned a great deal from his father, who had been a singer with the Chicago Opera.

Now that Max is gone, I look to find the great singers, like Josh Groban; like a countertenor I have found who sings at St. John the Divine—a man with a voice like an angel. This anonymous singer is a great artist, hidden in the veil of voices that can briefly free me, and many others, from our pain and trouble—in the great spaces at this church.

That is the purpose of singing, to lift the heart.

As we move forward in our lives, it is important that we remain open to new ways of doing things, and to learning new things. It's easy to shut out new things, especially as we get older, but learning can help us see better, work smarter, and be happier. We are all students, we are learning all the time, in traditional and nontraditional ways. One of the most traditional ways is to take a course, as I did when I learned to play the cello, and although I do not play the cello today, the times I spent with that wondrous instrument, and talking with my teacher, Robert Sylvester, meant a great deal to me.

Learning is something I feel I need to do throughout my life.

I went into therapy in 1963 in New York, after I had moved from Connecticut. Ralph Kline, the psychologist I was to see for the next seven years, told me to write down my dreams and keep a journal, and slowly that became a lifetime habit. My first journals, filled with dark thoughts, were tentative and hesitant and I had no conviction about anything I had written. I had to learn that the notebooks full of dreams and dark poems and strange journeys were leading me to another plateau of creativity.

In 1966, I showed one of my notebooks to my friend Bruce Langhorne. I was so afraid to show Bruce the book. Bruce was a close friend, a musical companion. He was a guitarist who had played for me and many other singers. He had traveled with me and Mimi Farina and Arlo Guthrie on our trip to Japan and Hawaii in 1966, after Dick Farina's death. I felt very close to him though we were not what I would call close friends. But I was a loner, except with my therapist and perhaps a friend or two. Bruce had lost some of his fingers in an accident when he was a child, playing with firecrackers. He played beautifully in spite of this loss, and I felt very comfortable with him and thought he might understand.

Still, I was petrified of what I was going to show him, and what I wanted to ask him. He lived in White Plains in an apartment with a balcony, and I drove from Manhattan in a rented car to see him. I shivered as I handed him my notebook—the dark writings frightened me, and I stepped out onto the balcony, afraid of his reaction. I was barely breathing when he called me back into the room to tell me what he thought of my writing.

Bruce was kind. He told me to go home and write five songs about a relationship.

I drove back to Manhattan and sat down at my piano. I thought about love and loss as I ran my fingers over the cool keys. My cats, Moby and Clyde and Jam, settled on the piano bench beside me, purring away.

I wrote my first song in about forty minutes, "Since You've Asked." Those forty minutes changed my life, and, at least for a while, the pain receded.

To learn is to live joyously and completely. The learning I do today will help me form and carve out the coming years. The lessons in the learning are not only of what I may be studying and what I may be absorbing, but affect every aspect of my life. Learning is living, learning is seeing, learning is being.

Learning is how we grow.

What I'll give you since you've asked
Is all my time together
Take the rugged sunny days
The warm and Rocky weather
Take the roads that I have walked along
Looking for tomorrow's time
Peace of mine

As my life spills into yours
Changing with the hours
Filling up the world with time
Turning time to flowers
I can show you all the songs
That I never sang to one man before

We have seen a million stones lying by the water
You have climbed the hills with me
To the mountain shelter
Taken off the days one by one
Setting them to breathe in the sun

Take the lilies and the lace
From the days of childhood
All the willow winding paths
Leading up and outward
This is what I give
This is what I ask you for
Nothing more

Collaborating

*F*inding people to easily collaborate with can take a lifetime, or a moment. A supportive collaborator can come in the form of a friend, a companion, a business partner, a lover, or even a stranger.

The stranger may seem to be the most unlikely, but can often be very important and instrumental in the creative process. He or she may harbor the dreams we dare not even speak. Almost everyone in your life was a stranger once, and perhaps the one you do not know is someone you can work with easily and learn from, and may even become your soul mate.

Michael Thomas was an important collaborator in my life. He is an Australian I met in London in 1966, and he came to live with me in New York. Michael was brilliant and funny and helped me to further my writing. Michael was with me when I first heard Leonard Cohen's songs, and was actually the one who said "Suzanne" was the song that would become a great hit, and that I should sing it, along with the song I immediately loved, "Dress Rehearsal Rag." But Michael and I drifted apart in the mid-sixties, as the pressures of travel and our different styles of life compromised the feelings I think we always had for each other.

It was the summer of 1968 and I was recording my eighth album for Elektra Records, the company I had begun making albums for seven years before. I had my first hit that year, my recording of Joni Mitchell's "Both Sides Now." That album was called *Wildflowers,* and contained the first of my writing—"Since You've Asked," "Skyfell," and "Albatross."

Now I was in the studio at Elektra's offices in Los Angeles, making an album that would be called *Who Knows Where the Time Goes.* By the time we came to record the song "Who Knows Where the Time Goes," I had met an amazing artist and performer named Stephen Stills, who was playing guitar on the album.

I have always found the creative partnership of making a record to be inspiring. Since I choose my co-producers, they usually complement my own creative energies, and I, for the most part, respect the other person and share the journey of searching for songs, making decisions about musicians and shape of accompaniment, as well as the social aspects of doing a project in depth. You are with people for long periods of time in the studio, eating meals, taking breaks, talking, falling into an intimacy that is often unique to that onetime, special experience. The experience is like living on a movie set, though often for a shorter time, and breeds bonds of lasting friendship that may never be repeated, but are lifelong and have a special quality.

I moved out to L.A., rented a house in Laurel Canyon, with a swimming pool and a big living room where the band and I practiced each day, and where my son, Clark, could join me for a few weeks. It was summer, and he was out of school in Vancouver, where he was still living with his father. I had lost custody of him when he was five. Now he was eight, and in these years I arranged many trips and visits so that we could have time together.

My producer on *Who Knows Where the Time Goes* was my old friend Mark Abramson. The band consisted of Gene Taylor, a tall, African-American bearded giant who had played bass with me on the road for years; Susan Evans, who was still very young and had gone on the road with me playing drums when she was under eighteen and needed a note from her mother; and Michael Sahl, long-haired and wild-eyed, a composer from New York who played great piano and had been with me for two or three years. The band came, and also Clark came to spend the summer with me.

We worked on the songs at the house in Laurel Canyon, swam with Clark in the pool, socialized at night and got ready to make a record on La Cienega Boulevard in the white stucco building that was Elektra's home on the West Coast. It was during those weeks that Robert Kennedy was killed in a hotel in Los Angeles, after Martin Luther King had been murdered a few weeks earlier. It was a painful time; a momentous time, I thought.

For the first sessions, we gathered in the studio among the colored rugs and the redwood sound dividers, eating chiles rellenos and drinking red wine, doing take after take of the songs I had chosen—"My Father," "Bird on the Wire," "First Boy I Loved," "I Pity the Poor Immigrant." After a few days of recording, David Anderle, who was running Elektra for Jac Holzman, and who had remixed "Both Sides Now," turning it into a hit, decided that he wanted to take over the production of the album. David had become a close friend when I worked on *Wildflowers*, and I trusted his opinion. Working with David meant I would not be working with Mark Abramson, the producer with whom I had made my past few albums. With Mark I had challenged the traditional folk style of my first recordings, which was to search out singer-songwriters like Tom Paxton, Eric Andersen, Pete Seeger, Mimi and Dick Farina. His energy and vision had been incredibly important in making *In My Life*, the album that helped me break out of the "folksinger" category into which I had originally fallen. *In My Life* included material from the Beatles, Bertolt Brecht, and Leonard Cohen.

I had met Leonard and heard his music with Michael Thomas before Leonard really hit it big, and, thanks in part to Michael, I recorded "Suzanne" and "Dress Rehearsal Rag"; it was also Leonard who had told me to start writing songs. A few weeks after the release of *In My Life*, I asked Leonard to perform on a benefit for WBAI, the public radio station in New York City, assuring him that he would enchant audiences with his beautiful songs. After a bumpy start in which he walked offstage during a performance of "Suzanne" and I came back out and sang the song with him, Leonard's career as a performer was launched, to the joy of audiences around the world.

Mark and I had put these songs together on *In My Life*, as well as songs from the *Marat-Sade* by Peter Brook with music by Richard Peaslee. We had also defied definition and broken more traditional boundaries by making *Wildflowers*, which used only orchestration, with no "folk" arrangements to be found on the entire album. To Mark's credit he handled the situation with great professionalism. He bowed to David's request that David take over the production of *Who Knows Where the Time Goes*, and went back to New York to await the outcome of this experiment of mine and Elektra's. *Who Knows Where the Time Goes* became a very successful album. And it also added a dimension to my career that would be life-changing for me, to say the least.

David had a plan for the album I was working on. Instead of relying on the musicians I had toured with and the studio players from Los Angeles, he would mix it up, bringing in an unusual group to work with me, which included Buddy Emmons, the great Nashville pedal steel player; Chris Ethridge, a bass player who had played with many rock groups; Jim Gordon, drummer extraordinaire from L.A. (who later murdered his mother with a hammer, in a cocaine blackout); and Stephen Stills, the great singer and guitarist who had recently broken up Buffalo Springfield and was looking to form a new group that would later become Crosby, Stills & Nash.

There was a sweetness about Stephen, but he was like a steel wire, wound up tight. His guitar playing had fire and sadness, and was just the thing for many of the songs on the album we were making. We made hot music together, and began a hot love affair. Too hot to last, it would turn out, but not too hot to create beautiful music.

You have many houses, one for every season
Mountains in your windows, violets in your hands

Thru your English meadows your blue-eyed horses wander
You're in Colorado for the spring

When the winter finds you, you fly to where it's summer
Rooms that face the ocean, moonlight on your bed
Mermaids swift as dolphins paint the air with diamonds
You are like a seagull as you said

Why do you fly bright feathered sometimes in my dreams?
The shadows of your wings fall over my face
I can feel no air, I can find no peace
Brides in black ribbons, witches in white
Fly in thru windows, fly out thru the night

Why do I think I'm dying sometimes in my dreams?
I see myself a child running thru the trees
Searching for myself, looking for my life
Looking everywhere crawling on my knees
I cannot see the leaves, I cannot see the light

Then I see you walking just beyond the forest
Walking very quickly, walking by yourself
Your shoes are silver; your coat is made of velvet
Your eyes are shining; your voice is sweet and clear
"Come on," you say, "come with me, I'm going to the castle"
All the bells are ringing, the weddings have begun

But I can only stand here—I cannot move to follow
I'm burning in the shadows and freezing in the sun

There are people with you living in your houses
People from your childhood who remember how you were
You were always flying, nightingale of sorry
Singing bird with rainbows on your wings

For about a year Stephen and I managed to do pretty well, though Stephen said he hated therapy, and New York. And I lived in New York and was in therapy. I was forever trying to find out how to be happier, do better work, not drink so much. Stephen had his own problems, but none of them had to do with creating. He made music as easily as most people fall out of bed. He would write a song a day, and found all the angst about creating to be a waste of his time. He was a truly amazing, moving, stirring guitar player, and a beautiful singer. He was thin as a whip, sexy as a dream, and said he was in love with me.

And I couldn't take the heat or the expectations, and soon we parted, but not before he put our romance into a song, which he recorded with Crosby, Stills & Nash on their first album. He came to the hotel I was staying at in Los Angeles, sat down on a couch of the Holiday Inn, and sang me the song. With his beautiful hands on the guitar and his blue eyes on mine, he sang me all the verses and choruses of the song that was to become "Suite: Judy Blue Eyes." It was a song that was meant to woo, and it broke my heart, and I sat and wept in that sad little hotel room, but I knew I couldn't go on with him; that day was good-bye, in spite of the beauty of the song, and the beauty of Stephen.

Although it was Leonard Cohen who really began my song-writing, it was Stephen who coddled me through my first attempt at writing prose, outside of journals and liner notes. And before we parted for the first time, he came to New York and played guitar with me at Carnegie Hall. *Life* magazine followed us around on tour for a couple of weeks and took shots of us being romantic in the woods and playing songs together. Sometime during that year I put together my first songbook for Grosset & Dunlap, which included many of the songs I had recorded to date: "Maid of Constant Sorrow," "In the Hills of Shiloh," "Mr. Tambourine Man," "Suzanne," "Both Sides Now," and "My Father," among others.

I had a lot of help on the book, with my publishers and with Herbert Haufrecht, who did the arrangements for the songs in the book. But it was Stephen who encouraged me to write the "comments, instructions and personal reminiscences" that, for me, were really the beginning of my writing of memoir.

The songs I had written at that point were certainly autobiographical in nature: "My Father," "Since You've Asked," "Albatross." But now, for the first time, I really wrote about my family and my life, about what it was to be a singer, to have a story to tell; I wrote about my son, Clark, and my difficulties with marriage, divorce, and losing custody.

Some of the most important writing I did was in a hotel room at the Beverly Hills in Los Angeles that Stephen booked while he was recording his first album with Crosby, Stills & Nash. I sat alone in the swanky room and wrote about my dysfunctional family and my wonderful life. (They say the only family that is not dysfunctional is the one that has only one member!) Stephen had planned this Yaddo equivalent for me and for a week I wrote, and drank red wine, and tried to stay as sober as I could during the day.

Sometimes at the end of the day I would get in my rented car and drive to the studio, dropping into the sessions where Stephen, David, and Graham were working on the new album. Joni Mitchell was there occasionally because she was dating David Crosby at the time. Her songs, which I had already started to record, always made me weep and yearn to write more of my own.

At the end of the stay in L.A. I took my hard-won typewritten pages home and asked my friend Yafa Lerner if she would help me edit them. Yafa was one of Leonard's closest friends, so in a way Leonard had a hand in my first prose writing, as well.

The first chapter begins with a memory of my father:

In the darkness he would read to us,
His fingers thwarting blindness

With the sound of flesh on paper
Brushing underneath the fantasy
Like the sound of wind moving through the house;
He soothed our fear of the night
With sighing hands . . .
and later on;
. . . every day the man who had no vision
Read verses streaked and blurred with color,
Deserts full of calico and rainbow-costumed heroes
Quilted all his dark days.

I don't know if I have ever captured my father any more clearly than in those afternoons at the Beverly Hills Hotel, a few miles from where he used to work in Los Angeles.

From 1944 to 1949, Daddy had his radio show on CBS on Santa Monica Boulevard. My mother would sometimes put us all in the car to drive from our white stucco house at 11572 Mississippi Avenue to Colfax and on into Beverly Hills, past the neighborhood of the Beverly Hills Hotel, to take Daddy to his radio show, when we were out of school for the day and he still had to do his show, national holiday or not, rain or shine. To this day, when I get out of the airport at LAX en route from New York, and step into the sunlight (there is always sunlight!) I have a vivid sense of being swept into the past—the light, the cactus, the green swaying sweetgrass; La Cienega and the memories of Elektra in the old days, my father taking us to hear the

Cisco Kid on a Saturday morning at the radio studio, his upright figure marching down the street on Mississippi Avenue to greet his wife and children, over whose faces he ran his hands to "see" them more perfectly. And Stephen playing his sweet guitar, and plying his sweet way into my life. Setting me up at the Beverly Hills, to write my memories of my childhood in my songbook, to capture my eternal and ongoing portrait of my father.

Collaborating is part of being creative, and there are many people on the path who help us, encourage us, and often make our work shine in a different way. These people may be parents, friends, lovers, or even strangers, but being open to people will bring new thoughts and ideas into our lives.

They can help us figure out what we want to do
and help us to accomplish our dreams.

Chapter 10

Connecting

Clark, my son, two months old, was fast asleep in my arms. I tucked him into his crib and called Michael's Pub. Michael said, "Sure, come down tomorrow and sing for the Friday-night crowd. Let's see if they like folk music any better than I do." They did, and by Saturday morning I had a job. Five nights a week, a hundred dollars a week. It was a fortune to us. Peter quit his paper route and we moved out of the basement into a house aboveground beside a little river in a woodsy neighborhood in Boulder.

—Judy Collins, *Trust Your Heart,* 1987

he circus, and my career, had begun.

Connecting with creative people has been a part of the collaborative process. I have made a world of friends whose talents are vastly different from that original model of my family, and as diverse as a field of wildflowers— painters, singers, writers, physical trainers, meditators, teachers, composers, lawyers, doctors. My friends are a constant reminder of the creativity of my life, my environment of thriving, eager, and thoughtful people, many more than were in my original family and just as creative and diverse.

All of them have different ways of working, and all of them have helped me in some way to learn, and to improve, my own way of working. To connect, to collaborate, to be in the river of your own and others' creativity, is to absorb the lessons you need to learn about your own process.

Susan Sontag wrote a wonderful novel called *The Volcano Lover*. It is one of the best novels I have ever read. I wrote to her after I read it, complimenting her work, and she told me later that for three years while she wrote it she didn't have any dates with people, didn't open her mail, didn't answer phone calls. She had to do this to get the book done. Having done so, she doubted whether she would be able to do another novel, as it had taken so much out of her life, since it caused her to stop connecting with her friends and her family.

Erica Jong lives in New York and has a home in Connecticut where she does most of her writing. She holes up in her studio in the country or in the city and works, but keeps her social life going, having dinner with friends, having time with her family. Erica's relationship with her work is one of complete immersion, but at the same time she stays involved in her life as the work goes on. Yet Erica told me recently that she had always approached her work as though it were a sentence from the SS, as though she were in prison every moment that she was writing. She has said, as many of us have, that creativity is often just pure struggle.

But recently Erica had a revelation about her work—that it might possibly be fun, and not necessarily a sentence as she previously thought. Even an accomplished, successful, published writer can learn new techniques and have a happier, more joyous time creating.

This is what I aspire to do—keep my life going as I work. I, too, am learning that they do not have to be separate from one another.

Gay Talese is married to my first editor, Nan. Nan edited Gay's books for many years. I love this couple and admire them both. Gay writes in the downstairs apartment of their New York brownstone. I have had a glimpse of his work space, a room with a desk and a chair and a wall filled with hundreds of tiny, minutely written index cards on which he is outlining whatever book he may be writing at the time. (I always find someone's work space as exciting as going to see the Chrysler Building—sheer excitement at seeing the most important landmarks of all, where art is made!)

When I call before noon, I will get the answering machine, Gay's or Nan's bright voice, a welcome to leave my name and number, and I will get a return call before the end of the day. On mornings at their beach house, Gay will not appear for breakfast, only a cup of coffee, but will be up for lunch and for a walk on the beach or a stroll down the main street. At night in New York we may see the Taleses for a laughter- and joy-filled dinner at a local restaurant, or share our deepest concerns about the state of the world with a few close friends. The work goes on, and life goes on, no matter what the creativity of the morning, or the artistic preoccupation of the afternoon. But life is fuller when we make the time to connect with people.

My friend Susan Cheever teaches writing at Bennington, writes books (most recently, *My Name Is Bill W*) and columns for *Newsday* and magazines like *Vogue*, as well as *Architectural Digest* and other publications. She writes beautifully and engagingly, and all the time. Her life is writing, and she covers the subjects that come up in her life—children, current social issues, the things that interest her and that she is engaged in. I always tell Susan I think she finds out what she thinks about things as she writes; her writing has a transparent, liquid quality about it, a sort of shimmer. Of course, she is the daughter of John Cheever, and the genes are pure and real, and relevant, I think. I find her life embraced by writing. Her process always inspires me, and teaches me.

Julia Cameron is a friend I have known for many years, but have seen a lot more of recently. Julia wrote one of the most important books in the creative learning library, called *The*

Artist's Way. Many of the things she recommends I had already been doing when I first read her book, such as writing my morning "pages," having learned their importance early on. However, as the journal took on a more prominent place in my life, I have learned much from Julia's writing on creativity and have personally shared with her many days of both agony and celebration over the demands of the creative life.

In 1971, I started a work group with a few friends, artists from different disciplines. In it were Cynthia MacDonald, a published poet as well as a teacher of poetry at Sarah Lawrence College; Susan Crile, a successful New York painter, well known and shown in many museums and collections; Al Levine, another published poet from New York; John Gruen, a successful painter; and me. I had just begun writing songs. I had written the first autobiographical pieces for publication, in a songbook as well as the liner notes for albums. I had come out of the privacy of journals and dreams and dark thoughts. I was beginning to see that I could, and must, do more of my own creative work, and the group was a great help in bringing out my creative habits and my fears, my joys and surprises.

By that year I had made nine or ten albums, had some number one hits. My son, Clark, was living with me, finally, in New York, and I was home more, trying to balance my creative life with single motherhood. Clark was difficult, and we were both in therapy with the Sullivanians, the therapists I had found in 1963, and with whom I would continue until 1975. I was drinking a lot, and still had seven or eight years to go before I would be able to quit. I was not as ill with the disease as I would become, and my round-the-clock drinking had not yet started. I drank every day, but you know, I could have stopped if I had wanted to.

It's just that I didn't want to. Right!

Stacy Keach and I were living together then. I had been in an encounter therapy group and taken some classes during my twenties. I had taken painting classes from Susan Crile, getting very drunk while I was down on the floor creating still-life paintings of fruit and vegetables and flowered Turkish plates, balancing the vodka with the acrylics, trying to remember not to put my brush in my drink. But the group was different.

We met each week at one another's homes in New York; we would have a simple meal, and read or show our work to the group. The person whose home we were in was "on." He or she would take us through a work in progress; talk about what was motivating the work. Mostly we listened, but we also celebrated, critiqued, and appreciated one another. It was a time of eagerness and nervous tension, and I would find myself working to finish a song so that I would have something to show when the meeting was at my home. That group helped me focus my work process and get over my fear of showing others my work before it was complete. Many people will not show work in progress under any circumstances, but I find it is wonderfully helpful and very exciting. It opens the work up for me, taking it out of the secret place where I worry and fret that things are not good enough. Criticism is a big help, unless is it mean-spirited.

In 1972, while the work group was still meeting, I rented a house on Long Island and began to write every day. The house was the last house on the beach in Amagansett, just before the dunes began. It was large and roomy with a studio/cottage out back where I could have the overflow of guests and friends who came out to stay for a few days through the summer. I stocked the kitchen with Zabar's coffee and fruits and vegetables bought in the fresh produce markets in town, unpacked my summer shirts and shorts, and canceled all the concerts my agent had booked for the summer.

This year, I was not going to travel. I counted up my money, made the decision to forgo income so I could spend the entire time writing, and had my Steinway piano shipped out.

I had done some good writing that year in the work group, and now, each day I got up and had my coffee and went to the piano and watched the waves pound on the Long Island coastline, hovering over my lyrics and trying to put words to music. I had started painting by then, and had found that link between the color and the form of still life and the sound of music in my head. I was in heaven, truly engaged in the practice of letting go and letting the music come.

Clark spent time at the beach house that summer, when he was not at camp or visiting his father in Canada, and I was still having a relationship with Stacy, who came out to the beach house from time to time. My sister Holly came for a few days, friends from the city, including my work group, with whom I had a session. The Hamptons were not the socially swinging place they are today, and life was slower and easy and mostly about work during the day, and socializing at night with just a few friends, or going to Gozman's fish restaurant on the docks in Montauk, for lobsters and mussels, or sitting around the porch looking out at the ocean, eating grilled fish and drinking tall vodkas.

I got to know a wonderful poet named Kenneth Koch, who took me to his house in the middle of a potato field and fed me a new potato just out of the ground for dinner. It was one of the best things I have ever tasted.

The days went by like a string of saltwater pearls, and I was tan and very fit, eating fresh corn and fresh fish and seeing friends occasionally for visits and talks about creativity. My friends Susan and Cynthia came out to see me. We shared our new work, songs, sketches, ideas, and talked of writing and singing and how they all connected.

○

So many people have helped the connections to my work: the co-director of my movie about Antonia Brico, Jill Godmillow; Coulter Watt, the cameraman on *Antonia*; the men and women who have played on my albums, instrumentalists, conductors, orchestraters; the lovers in my life who have told me I could when I thought I couldn't; the producers of many of my albums, the people I have co-written songs with. There are many others whom I've worked with and connected with who have been infinitely helpful in my life.

For you, it may be the person who edits your books; it may be the person or people who write the music for the dance you have choreographed; the person who designs the cover for your latest book. There are so many people who help us.

Believing in the myth that an artist works on his or her own, and owes nothing to anyone else, is a common illusion. People help us all the time—to realize our dreams, to put our best work into the best light, and to realize our potential and our value to the world.

Connecting to others feeds creative life and reminds me once again that in my creative adventures, there are moments when I must find seclusion in order to be creative.

The truth is, we are never really alone.

Chapter 11

Hoping

ope is the secret behind the secret. I find it in the shifting of a circumstance that I thought could never change, in the belief that life keeps on rolling; trees keep on putting out leaves in the spring; little animals keep on begging to be cuddled, hoping for the best from you, giving their best. Babies smile, hoping for the best. I smile, hoping for the best.

I believe the best is yet to come. When I am on the floor with bitter tears and sorrows, I pray and meditate, praying mostly for hope. Hope will get you through anything. And hope comes in at the window on the darkest day, in the most bitter of times.

Leonard Cohen says,

> *"There is a crack in everything,*
> *that's how the light gets in."*

Hope is important when we create, but bliss, destruction, passion, light, misery are all part of the creative act as well. To create, we must be willing to destroy perceived ideas and go beyond expectations, ours as well as others'.

Picasso said,

> *"Every act of creation is first of all*
> *an act of destruction."*

I have to destroy my idea of what is right or what other people expect of me. To make something new, I must let the new idea live; kill the Buddha on the road. Look for new answers to the old questions, and hope to find something else, something other than what might be expected.

What *does not* work? Negativity, expecting the worst, seeing the dark side, seeing the glass as half empty. Of course, there is nothing like the feeling of being immersed in a project. I feel I am truly in a creative state when working every day is easy and seems to come naturally, and I am in a timeless, spaceless place where I can focus; that heavenly space where the path is very clear, and the concentration magical.

Every day we are confronted with the creativity of nature, how the flowers bloom, how creatures die and are born. All the glory of creativity we experience is celebrated and lauded in churches and ceremonies around the world, in dances and songs, in the miracle of scripture and revelations; everywhere we see and are a part of the creative stuff of our universe, our planet, our earth.

It is natural to create. Humans have been creating since before we even had language. Making a picture on a cave wall to show what happened, how the buffalo was slain, the lion captured, the prey brought down. Making clothes, utensils, drawings, and using these things to help create a home on a sometimes strange and scary planet.

I have been following my creative bliss for most of my life, and it has not always been an "easy" path. I find, looking back on this path, that the road of creativity is forever unfolding for me every day I live, and that it is not an unusual or strange or exotic way of thinking and being, but natural. Creativity is natural to all of us.

In 1994, I was asked to be a spokesperson for UNICEF, the organization that works with children in 162 countries around the world. I went to meet with the president of UNICEF, Jim Grant, who had been with the organization for sixteen years at that time. UNICEF's offices are on East Forty-sixth, near the United Nations buildings on the East River, a honeycomb of international activity where Africans, Irishmen, Canadians, Russians, and an international set gather to help take care of the needs of children around the world.

UNICEF was started after World War II to ensure that the children of war-devastated countries had proper nutrition, medical care, and education. The organization is known for its clearheaded finances (it has to raise its own money and is not funded by the UN) and its total devotion to girls and boys around the world.

Jim Grant was tall and thin, a handsome man who reminded me a bit of Henry Fonda or maybe Scott Glenn in his younger days. He had a big, welcoming smile and the vivacious, inspiring personality of a man whose job is to change the world and make you want to help him. He talked about his beloved organization and the work they did around the world with passion and at the same time with humor. Then he leaned across the table and looked at me with cobalt blue eyes that were full of light. In his hand he held a little piece of white stuff, maybe an inch in diameter.

"This costs twenty-five cents," he said, "and it can save a child's life." The hydration salts were being used by UNICEF all over the world to help save the lives of hundreds of thousands of children suffering and dying from dehydration. "We have saved millions of lives with it so far."

Then he asked me to look at a book of children's art that had been put together from the drawings of children in refugee camps, hospitals, and neighborhoods devastated by the war in Bosnia and Croatia. He told me what UNICEF was doing in the former Yugoslavia—psychological programs designed to save children from the fallout of land mines, war, starvation, and the ravages of war. The program had been started in Mozambique by a Norwegian, Rune Stuvland, who saw in art the means of saving children's emotional lives and helping them through the trauma of war.

He pulled out a book with the title *I Dream of Peace,* and flipped open the pages. Drawings made by children, simple line drawings with bright colors of red, blue, and green, houses on fire, burning villages, helicopters in flames, bullets flying through the air, refugees in long lines filing out of town over the mountains. These images filled the pages, until the end of the book, when the pictures became personal and sunny, full of flowers and smiling faces of the same children.

"This tells the story, their own, and lets them know that they can survive, if we give them a little hope. Art gives them hope."

The book, he said, was being published the following week and UNICEF had a spot on the *Today* show to launch it. I asked him if I could help. He nodded.

"I want you to write a song about these children," he said. "And sing it on the show."

"By Monday?" I asked, and he nodded.

It was three o'clock on Thursday afternoon.

"Of course," I answered, and by Monday I had the song and sang it on the *Today* show. Harry Smith was on that show, and the words were so new that I read them off a sheet of paper, wearing my reading glasses. But I had the song; it had come in hours, literally, in the two or three days before the show. They showed the book of children's art—beautiful, heartbreaking pictures that were made by the children in Bosnia and Croatia, in refugee camps, hospitals, and schools; the story on paper of flame burning out of buildings, refugees wandering over the mountains, planes dropping bombs on citizens, tanks rolling through small towns—the awesome, terrifying landscape of fear and torment that these children were living in. I was crying; I don't how I got through the performance. "Song for Sarajevo" was finished, dedicated to the children in a world that had turned into a deadly place where it was often certain death to be a child.

Blood in all the streets running like a flood
There's no where to hide, no where I can go
I reach out my hand touching death itself
Just another holy day in Sarejevo

I can hear my heart pounding like a clock
Hiding from the planes and from the bombing

Fire in the sky burning down my life
There is no more love and no more longing

But when I close my eyes
I dream of peace
I dream of flowers on the hill
I dream I see my mother smiling
When I close my eyes I dream of peace

After writing the song, I made two trips to the region of the former Yugoslavia, and actually met with one of the young boys who had made such a moving painting for *I Dream of Peace*.

We sat out on a terrace in Dubrovnik, while the sound of bombing came to us over the sea, and talked and cried together. He was going to live, he said, in Italy, where his family had decided to settle since the war was still going on.

Sadly, Jim Grant lived only a year or so after our first meeting. I saw him a few more times. My hopes for a long and lasting friendship with Grant ended, along with his family's and UNICEF's hopes, with his death from cancer very soon after our meeting about the launching of *I Dream of Peace*. The song is really for Jim, and his great work with UNICEF. Carol Bellamy is now the executive director of UNICEF in New York and is doing a splendid job, and would make Jim proud and glad for all her energy and devotion to his passion.

I went to a party for the firefighters in New York in the spring of 2002. It was a gathering of friends and families of those who had died in the tragedy at the Towers in New York. Many of these were rescue workers, firemen and -women who had been in the teams at Ground Zero looking for their friends, sometimes finding them, a terrible experience, and, worse, more often not finding any sign of their lost comrades. I didn't think I could, or would, ever write anything about the events of 9/11. Too terrible to contemplate, too awful to re-see, re-feel, re-experience.

That night Ronan Tynan, Kevin Bacon, Chris Botti, and many others were gathered to make some music, share some food, and just get together for what was hoped would be a social night, a night of friends getting together, a night to honor the dead but also to honor the living. I felt privileged to meet a number of the firefighters, and their families.

They are a great section of society, those who fight our fires and respond to our calls for help, who sometimes save our lives and often witness our domestic scenes and our failings, but more often attest to our bravery in situations of personal distress and need. Having a close family, as I do, and a number of siblings, I had the feeling that they, too, were part of my family. They have strong friendships, loyalty beyond the call, a social order that is beaten out of the necessities of the job.

That night I simply felt honored to be in the presence of such extraordinary people, who had saved three thousand lives and had to live through the aftermath, the back draft, of that awful day. We all had some food, chatting and getting to know one another. A number of the guys from my local firehouse on the Upper West Side came by to say hello. The mayor spoke, the head of the union spoke, and Kevin Bacon played, Chris Botti played. Ronan sang with his sweet Irish tenor. His niece from Ireland was there, a seventeen-year-old who was on her first visit to the United States. I sang "Amazing Grace," and then joined the crowd for coffee and dessert. A lot of guys came up to me and showed me a tattoo on the back of their necks, exposing the tender flesh under a shirt collar so I could see the number 343. The number of firefighters lost on 9/11.

In the days following the party, I couldn't get the image out of my mind, the thought of the tattoo, the thought of the tragedy. I kept bringing it up, with friends and with my husband, till he said to me, "I think you have to write about this."

Usually I find that when I sit at the piano and noodle, something will come—a melody, a few words—and often I will put it on the tape recorder, as I do in my regular songwriting sessions, and let it roll while I fumble and noodle and sing my heart out. About this night, I had to simply sit quietly with a pad of paper and write it out and the story poured off my pen.

A few days later, I went to the firehouse in my neighborhood uptown and was able to sing the song for the guys, share a meal, and laugh and cry with them. It is a moment I will never forget.

To Kingdom come, to hell and gone
To somewhere far away
Where murder doesn't break the heart
On a sunny day
    —Chorus of "Kingdom Come"

Hope springs eternal, they say. As long as I can hope, I can find my way somehow. As long as we can hope, we can see around the edges of life as they appear, and look for the best, look for the love, look for the light. It is no longer the responsibility of the world around us to make us happy; it is our responsibility to create joy in our lives—and we must take what happens to us under all circumstances, and find a way to tell the story, to find the way through the dark, to get through to our own strength from the failings that come to everyone, no matter how strong or how gifted they are.

Chapter 12

Imagining

W hen I started therapy in 1963, at the age of twenty-four, the first thing I was told by my therapist was that I should write down my dreams. I remember much of what I dream, and what is lost is never lost; or so I believe, if I try to remember where I have been, even a little. Dreaming helps my imagination, and I have heard that if you have lived twenty years, you have enough material from your dreams and your memories for a lifetime of writing and creating, even if you were to have no more dreams or memories at all. I am sure teenagers have long memories—even at eleven or fifteen, I know I did!

Imagining, remembering, and dreaming are closely related. Each fits into the puzzle, a piece of the whole that contributes to creative thoughts and actions. I dreamed when I was in my late twenties that my onetime lover Stephen Stills came to see me. I asked him how he was, and he began in a long monologue to tell me. I awoke realizing that he had never asked me how I was. Then he wrote "Suite: Judy Blue Eyes" for me.

I wrote my dream down, shivering in its memory. I was working on songs in my studio and went to the piano, sat down, and began to play the melody that the dream had set up in my mind and my heart. The lyrics came later, fused with the aching loss of that splendid, short, forever important love affair of the heart. The song is called "Houses." He has never known, I do not think, that it is for him.

There were times when my most haunting dream was try-ing to fly and not being able to get off the ground, running along the earth as though I were a winged creature, reaching out with my wings, and failing to make it into the air. That dream repeated itself into my thirties, but I remembered that first dream, I knew I could fly, and when I was in my twenties, in love, and in therapy, making records of music and loving the music, I began to dream that I was flying. It took no effort to get off the ground, to sail on the wind, to make it over the fence, to try for the heavens.

Things I've heard that help me:

- Sometimes the good is the enemy of the best.
- Follow your heart, but remember to start.
- Any road will get you there as long as you take the steps.
- What do you love? Do it.

When I sit at the piano and begin to play, something happens to my memory and my sense of poetry. I am drawn into my imagination, where all my storytelling begins. The melody and the words come together, but it is my fingers on the keys that trigger the poetry. I sit as if in a kind of trance, one in which I am happiest, and most creative. Sitting at the piano, I am in a kind of heaven on earth.

A good exercise for the memory and imagination is to write everything you remember about, say, your aunt Edith.

What was she wearing that day she came to bring you your birthday present? (I imagine a white jacket, buttoned to the throat; black shoes, simple and sensible. She has a handbag of blue leather, not fancy but quality workmanship; her handkerchief, which she brings to her nose from time to time, is of flowered silk that matches her purse. Her hat has a veil that she pulls down over her eyes as she is leaving.)

What did she smell like? (Lily of the Valley)

What did she say—to you, to your mother, to your father? (Here is another story—a family quarrel, the first meeting in twenty years, a falling-out over money? Does she actually talk to your parents, or only to you?)

Where did she sit? (Next to you, with her back to your mother? Why?)

What did you eat? Where did you eat? (She did not eat; lunch sat getting cold at the table and you felt bad for your mother, who had cooked chicken and potatoes and baked a cake for the occasion. But you didn't tell your mother; you were not speaking to her at the time.)

Imagining is a bit like dreaming while you are awake.

There is the story of Faulkner, I think it was, staring out the window in his studio. His wife comes in and begins to speak to him about something—dinner, the children, the weekend to come—and he snaps at her not to interrupt him. She says, "But you were just staring out the window!" and he replies, "Yes, staring is one of the most important ways I work!" I am assuming this was at the start of their marriage, and that she learned fast!

I remember much of my childhood, either from my real memory or from having been told a great deal about myself as a child.

I was born on the first of May, the day of the celebration of socialism and of the rebirth of nature. I listened as if mesmerized as my mother and father sang to me as they walked me to sleep. I can remember the yearning that sprung into being even at three or four, wanting to play a certain piece of music because of the way it sounded when I played it on the piano, wanting to hear my father sing a certain song I had fallen in love with.

It is a good idea to use what comes to you, in memory and in real life, in your imagining.

Imagining will let us in on our own secrets, and will take us to places we need to go. Let's do things that stimulate our imagination—walking, talking to friends, going to a concert. There are times when nothing is more stimulating to my imagination than sitting in a beautiful theater, hearing music or seeing a play. I let my mind wander, my imagination roam.

That is what art and nature are for,
letting our imaginations run wild!

Chapter 13

Releasing and Revising

They say if you hold on to resentment,
you are the one who is poisoned.

—Traditional saying

How does your work become yours?
How do you find the things that make what you do
unmistakably yours?
How do you find your voice?

*H*olding on to anger or resentment, fear or worry or the memory of a bad review or the slight of a friend can be incredibly detrimental. I must release these things in order to be free to work well and to live well. There is nothing more painful than to have a resentment floating around in my head, waking me up at night, putting me out of sorts. I have techniques to remove these things from my mind and to release any self-deprecating thoughts I may have as well. Releasing negative thoughts and feelings makes each day better, even if I am not getting any work done at all.

A mind clear of anger and fear is, for me, the best place to work, but it is a discipline to release these negative thoughts and swirling demons that are my enemies, these doubts that stand in my way. But I can do it, and you can, too. It just takes a little work.

Take a walk. Make a phone call to a friend,
take a bath, pick up that book you were reading last
night and finish it. Banish the negative; get in the
habit of refusing to listen to the committee who
thinks what you are writing is crap!

I find that I can release the pain of difficult things when I write about them. I have written a number of books in recent years, including a novel, and most recently a book about suicide. In the process of grieving and trying to get over my son Clark's death by his own hand, I met and became friends with a wonderful professor of thanatology, who started the first suicide hotline in the United States. Professor Edwin Schneidman is a brilliant man who has studied and taught at Harvard and is a professor emeritus at UCLA. Like my singing teacher Max Margulies, he is someone I like to talk to about process and art, for he knows more than most about those things, and is a great teacher and comfort.

He has many ideas about creativity. He told me recently that when you think about it, the thing that is terribly original about the music of Mozart is that it is so carefully formed, so heart-pulsingly predictable. "Mozart creates his own world and allows you to dance his dance, even if just for a little while. And you always know it is his music. Amadeus—literally meaning 'friend of God.' What a name!"

Having been trained first as an interpretive singer as well as a pianist, I often think about that part of my training and how it impacts the whole creative life. One singer can sing the entire repertoire of Mozart and make you weep with joy; another may make you want to run for the exit. So what is the difference? Why does the voice of Pavarotti make us weep with pleasure while another Italian tenor might make us wish we were deaf?

Pavarotti has said he learned early in his career that no matter what you do, half the people will hate you and the other half will love you. Or, as someone said to me recently, it's not your business who hates you and who loves you; it is your business to do your work in the best way possible, and let go of the results.

Creating is often letting go.

"Expect nothing and all will be velvet" is a phrase that sometimes helps me. And through the process of creating without expectation, without worrying about what others may or may not think of my work, I have found freedom, and I have come to know that all parts of my life are creative.

Revising is very much a part of releasing. There are times when the need for revising is absurdly evident and the process can be easy, and there are times when the necessary revisions are elusive, making it more difficult. The first draft, bad or good, is a powerful thing to get done, because then the real work can come. No first draft gets published, as far as I know, no matter how good it is. There is always major or minor tweaking, reorganizing, and slashing of some parts of my work that must be done, whether it is moving verses and images in the body of a song or rewriting a press release that had to go out "yesterday!" The TV special I make must be edited and re-formed, looked at again and again, minute or huge changes made. Revising happens in the hours during the later part of the day, and, for me, often follows lunch. I enjoy the fruits of my labor, the thoughts that drift out of the music I am writing, the words I am putting on paper.

When I am recording, there is usually a natural time when the musicians I work with take lunch, talk about their families, listen to the music we have recorded, talk, gossip about who we know in the business, what is going on, who is doing what.

And then the revising, reshaping, and perhaps even re-recording, begin. Releasing what does not work, reshaping what does, perhaps. Regretting nothing!

Making an album or a CD has changed only in the method

used to record, not in the kind of process needed to complete the task. Vocals have to be sorted out and comps of the vocals done, on grids that look like somebody's back porch screen, all lines and crosses, with words in between. I have to choose the takes of the song that have the vocals I want to hear; the tracks have to be cleaned up, a guitar part overdubbed, perhaps, or another instrument added. It is seldom that the one-take song makes it to a final CD. Rare, though it does happen. Most of recording, like writing, is inspiration assisted by revision.

There is much rewriting and editing that has to be done when I am in the throes of a book or a CD. I must listen to takes of the songs I have recorded and make the notes that will help me and my recording engineer and associate producer choose how to put together the results of a session. This is very like writing a book, in that there is editing and collaboration. The alone time is finished and now there are others involved with the work.

Afternoons, in and out of the studio, are the times I often use to revise a recording, or rework a song, or edit a manuscript. It's a good use of time because you want your fresh, new work to be done in the morning, if possible, and the technical, and often busywork, of revising and editing can be done in the later hours since it doesn't require the same sort of fresh inspiration.

Then there is the revising of where we are and where we want to go, who we are and how we can get comfortable about that, change bad habits, quit biting our nails or tearing out our hair. Revising my natural bent for self-destructive behavior is something I have worked on a great deal in my life. It is not that I was a bad first draft, but there certainly was work to be done, habits to form and to get rid of, and discipline to enforce.

My notebooks are filled with ideas, with two- and five- and ten-year projections; with lists of songs I want to learn, and put on albums; there are different kinds of albums I want to put together. I've noted the possibility of recording more collections of my favorite songwriters. Now that I have done a collection of Dylan and one of Cohen, there are a few others I would harness with my voice, only to let loose in the world so they are heard in a new way. My notebooks also contain poems that are complete but will probably never see print.

But I understand that the journals, the unfinished songs and poems, the trail of words and melodies that lie in my archival past, and present, are all keys to the creative life, the dialogue with the inner self, the daily and weekly reflections on every part of living that help me live my life.

Releasing, letting go of, editing, revising, all are part of the process of finding the final "product" and making it the best it can be. You might want to change the steps of a dance you are working on, after you see that they are better when organized in a different way; you may want to repaint a painting you are working on, or rephotograph something you love but don't think you got the best shot of. You may want to put all the chapters of a book on the floor and, as my friend Gloria Steinem suggests, get down and treat the chapters like the pattern for a dress, rearrange and restructure what you are doing. All this is part of releasing your hold on the thing itself, and letting its true pattern emerge. You sometimes are helping out by letting go. Let the thing breathe, take another look, let some time go by, and look again. Let go of what you thought your creative act was, so that it becomes what it should be: *perfectly imperfect. Imperfectly perfect.*

Night

A time to go out with friends, to go to a movie, to watch television and perhaps just think and read, to rest and light a candle, to pray for those you love as well as your enemies; a time of peaceful sleep, of rejuvenation. A time for dreams!

Chapter 14

Beginning Again

here have been many times in my life when I had to reinvent myself, moving in new creative directions, finding new avenues for my work, in both performing and writing as well as singing.

Beginning again, whether starting a new book, writing a new song, or taking on a new endeavor altogether, such as the speaking engagements that my writing has led me to, always entail putting new emphasis on what I do, building on what I know, and re-creating something that can be new, fresh, more interesting.

Beginning again is not starting from scratch. I think it is drawing on the strengths that are already there, making a bet that if I feel the desire for a change in my heart, the gods and goddesses will give me the means to accomplish that goal.

I am always looking for new songs, listening for what might interest me to write about, and thinking about how to stay afloat and recharge my work as a concert artist.

Music and food and performance were always in close proximity in my family. My mother was a formidable cook as well as a great tailor. Her creative life could be seen in savory casseroles, and the bread that she kneaded and baked once a week, as well as in the beautiful clothes she made. Our home was always filled with the smell of baked bread and Sunday dinners of chicken and dumplings and standing rib roasts, accompanied by browned new potatoes, or dreamy mashed potatoes lathered with butter; rolls she made from scratch; her famous cookies and the divinity candy she made in a pot on the stove and whipped by hand until recently, at eighty-eight, since she no longer has the strength in her hands to stir the divinity, at least in her cooking.

My father's creativity was what people noticed most, since it was public and brought us the money to buy the cloth for the clothes and the standing rib roasts for Sunday dinners. He was so filled with drama that people couldn't help but notice him first, not my mother, even though she was also incredibly creative, and a great cook, a wonderful mother, and the one who sewed the clothes and got the meals together and drove my father to many of the performances and read to us and put us to bed with hot tea when we were ill. But Daddy was bigger than life, and so you noticed him first.

The thought that what a woman did and what a man did might be equally important was not a fashionable thought in those days. The dignity of housework and childrearing and cooking was not acknowledged as it is now. But both my parents thought ahead of the times, and believed in social issues, like equality and women's rights, and had been politically active in their college years and continued to inform our education with ideas lofty and, they thought, practical.

In 1949, my father's contract at CBS radio in Los Angeles ran out. I remember we didn't have much money that year, but I also remember the Christmas of 1948 as being one of the happiest of my childhood, even though I know now that it was a tough time for my parents. The money was short and I think my father must have stopped drinking for a while, controlling his monster for those days after, as he would say, the ax had fallen. Before a new sponsor had appeared, there was an offer from Denver to come out and replace a radio personality named Happy Jack Turner who had died of a heart attack suddenly. They had scouted Daddy in the fall of 1948 and after he lost the job at CBS. Then they made an offer he couldn't refuse and offered to bring his family to Denver.

That last Christmas in Los Angeles I got a Mexican dancing doll and a bottle of New Mown Hay perfume and was as happy as a clam. The bad news was good news, for a new horizon beckoned.

We were taught to make the best of things, and create something happy out of whatever happened to us. These Christmases were part of my creative training. Daddy would write a poem with all of us contributing, a sort of group conscience effort that told of the joys of gratitude and celebration. Mother would buy colored construction paper and we would agree on a picture, and then the glue and the sparkles and the paint would come out. Mother would make a batch of her wonderful fudge, and we would gather around to put the cards together, scattering sparkle over the glue on the spots of snow, cutting the paper, drawing with our pots of paint.

When I was in my first year of college, living away from home at Mac Murray College in Jacksonville, Illinois, I found the separation from my family terribly painful. Jacksonville is a flat place, and when you look up against the wheat fields your eyes do not find mountains at the end of their gaze, nor the rolling foothills of the Flatirons, nor the tip of Long's Peak. There is just wheat, and that is about it. And red brick. The building I lived and went to school in was red brick, in contrast to the snow that winter, and to the wheat fields in the summer.

My mother, many years later, sent me the following story, which she had found and saved from my baggage on my grateful return the following spring to the mountains again.

The Plane Soldier

I boarded the broad-winged sky bird at La Guardia airfield on a Sunday evening, a year ago. June was ending, and the sun of that particular day poised on tiptoe at the edge of the horizon, peering out to see if the great black sky was ready to take over her night watch. I stepped up the stairs, bags in hand, my legs in their silky nylons still holding the warmth of the sun's parting. A wave of gloved hands and a final grin ushered me into the carpeted tube of the plane.

Security is a word I dislike using. It smacks of satisfaction and complacency. Still I must say that I felt secure, in this great bird as she swept the wind in back of her wings and bared her silver forehead in that mellow gold light. I touched the lever on my chair and leaned back to watch Manhattan Island loom up and then fall back against the sea. That's a beautiful thing. I had never seen it before. I said as much to the uniformed young man at my side; but when I turned to end the sentence with a "traveler's smile," as I like to call them, I knew that he had seen it many times. He began, then, to tell me of some of those times. The talk soon flowed between us.

As he talked, I had time to study the face under the khaki hat; the boy was still there, though the man was trying desperately to overthrow him. His smile was still the boy's smile, and there was a certain shyness that darted from his eyes as he raised them to gaze out the sky-window as he spoke. His skin was olive, deep-colored and smooth. His home, he told me, was on an island in the Philippines.

"There is death, now, in my house," he said. "Your Uncle Sam sends me home to weep at the funeral of my father. Sorrow, in the Army, warrants a twenty-day leave, you know."

The boy whose father had died and who had olive skin was called Andrew. We spoke now, as Andrew and Judy, about life in general and fathers in particular. His father had been a fisherman. I told him my father is not a fisherman and is not dead yet. He said he would hear of him, anyway. So spun the paternal conversation until the great lights of Chicago swung into view under our wings.

The steward announced we would refuel and reload in half an hour, so I got off to stretch, leaving my companion dozing in his chair.

I do not profess to be a cosmopolitan and, although I hear a great many of these people insist that Chicago's Midway Airport is a hole, I still find a great deal in the place that fascinates me. I left the plane, alone, and hustled around the horseshoe once, getting my bearings, and nearly losing my life to the taxis. I walked aimlessly inside, then, eyeing the vending machines and the snoring sailors. A few minutes before plane time, I spied a great mound of green boxes, each sporting a Marshall Field's sticker, and each, I knew, filled with "traveler's preservatives": ham and roast beef sandwiches and other assorted goodies. I bought two, and re-boarded the plane, prepared to surprise my young friend. Our seats were both empty, so I tucked my treasures under the seat and sat back to look out the window, nonchalantly.

The olive-skinned lad finally appeared as the propellers were being given the first manual thrust. He smiled and placed his hat and some packages on the rack above.

A few minutes later, when the plane was fully launched and the pleasant whir filled the compartment, a simultaneous presentation took place; I put my green Marshall Field's box in his lap with some phrase about our being hungry up here in the sky, and I found in my hand a bag of hot French fries and a hamburger. We worked out the culinary details, laughing, and both of us ate well all the way to Denver.

Home loomed before me, and I quite forgot about my friend Andrew in the rush of parents' faces and brothers' arms. Then I went home to a long, midnight chat with Mom and Dad, over steaming coffee and hash browns.

I didn't mention the young Philippine soldier, even when I thought of him again. But I will remember the olive-skinned fisherman's son for many a plane ride.

—*Judy Collins, Mac Murray College,*
Jacksonville, Illinois, 1958

The scene is the beginning of a set of stories of strangers that must have formed the background for "The Blizzard," which I wrote many years later. The theme once again tells me that all of us have things that haunt and follow us, inspire and delight us. We must just follow the stranger's path, for it will lead us home.

Don't be afraid of beginning again. You never start off without the memory of the past experience, anyway, and starting again can give you a new focus and a new purpose. I started my own record label, Wildflower Records, recently, and so feel that I am beginning again, but all the experience I have had in the past is coming to bear, and I am finding that this is the natural next step.

Beginning again is usually the next right thing, the next step in your journey, with a new view and new excitement and new challenges. You will be up to it. *You only need to start.*

Chapter 15

Struggling

*S*uccess often looks easy, as though it dropped out of the sky onto an artist you may know. A closer look will usually tell us that no one, not even the most gifted and the most successful of artists, has it easy all the time. There are moments of total pain and agony in any creative life, and I have experienced many of them, as I will continue to. Struggle is one of the prices of the joys and pleasure of living the creative life, on both a personal and a professional level.

Many times my contracts with recording companies and publishers have been dropped; many times I have received terrible reviews of things I think are wonderful; many times I have received rejection notices for books I have written. I like to hear stories about writers whose books are great successes but who once experienced nothing but pink slips, sometimes for years, because that gives me hope. Not every publisher is the right one, not every record label is the right one—and sometimes finding the right one can take years. Success is not the first thing on the horizon, if you are looking for that, and yet, believe in the process and you will win. Stay the course and you will win. Get used to being the answer to your own prayers, and you will be.

I drank for twenty-three years. After getting sober in 1978, and not having written much of anything for about four years, I yearned to write, yearned for the songs to spill out, as my friend Jules Fiffer said they would, like birds flying out of my hands. I was working on my journals, as usual, but the freewheeling writing was not coming easily, even as I began to heal and to move ahead again in my singing career, making a new album with Charles Koppelman, one of the great producers in the music business.

Through some mutual friends who had studied with him, I found a great teacher. Ira Proof created a method of reaching your inner stories by working with dreams and memories, interweaving the experiential with the dreaming, the autobiography with the storytelling, and the meditation with the actual writing. I found his workshop in 1979 after I had been in a deep funk creatively in which I had not a glimmer of an inspiration in four years of round-the-clock drinking. I had written two songs in 1973, "Song for Duke" and "Out of Control." Then, no songs for five years, while I drank myself into oblivion, ruining my serenity and my health. I had written the notes to my 1977 collection called *So Early in the Spring—The First Fifteen Years,* but that was about it, for the writing.

Also, just to show you that these troubles don't always make themselves clear on the outside, I was having the most "successful" period of my career to that point. I had my second top-ten hit, "Send in the Clowns," the year before, and had recorded *Judith,* an album that went platinum and still sells incredibly well, during the most difficult year of my drinking. That year, I was introduced to Ira's classes, held in those years at the New School for Social Research, in the Village in New York.

I chose a Saturday and Sunday session. I sat with other searchers and writers in a sunny conference room at the New School and began to write, using the cross-reference method that Ira proposes for stirring up the inner creative process. In the book he provides, I had created many sections, about childhood, memories and experiences, dreams and a chronology of my life. As I started to write, I could feel pay dirt under my hands—and as the afternoon progressed, I became more and more uncomfortable. I got up, took a walk around the room, and then, finally, I had to leave. I had a pain in my stomach that would not stop. It was as though a fist had punched a hole in my gut, I was literally bent over and made my way to the door. The friend who had brought me was concerned and followed me out to the street, where it had started to rain. She offered to take me home, but I told her I was fine. I wasn't! I made my way uptown, nearly howling with the pain.

Of course, I knew very well what had happened. Ira's method of getting to the core of things had broken through a deep wall of resistance, and the pain had to rush out, and get my attention. Either that or I had acute appendicitis and I didn't believe that for a moment.

I began writing, in a rush of songs. I had done some body work in my twenties and thirties—with a student of Alexander Lowen, who worked my joints and limbs free of much locked-up anxiety; with Ilana Rubenfeld, who is a healer and had taken me through many difficult physical periods; with yoga, meditation, est, and other forms of physical and emotional therapy—that I knew I was not having a massive hemorrhage of the physical kind. The rush of work and writing that came to me after that rainy afternoon when I left Ira's group session in terrible pain brought joys that cannot even be measured. I got to know Ira in the years following that afternoon, and even took another class from him. We talked about my "breakthrough," and he said he felt it was a natural physical reaction to all the pent-up pain of the drinking, when I had been unable really to work in a way that was free, and open, and creative.

I had always worked, of course, and in my twenties and thirties had been able to write songs and even a seven-chapter songbook of life memories, *The Judy Collins Songbook*. But now, sober, the real work began.

I was very receptive to Ira's approach. He suggested meditations, mantras that you created yourself, things that moved you and brought you in touch with your own memories and tactile sense of beauty. One of the Entrance Meditation mantras I wrote to begin my work each day was

". . . In this sea the touch of the water heals my fear."

"Under the eaves I can hear the sound of rain."

"In the shadows there are snowflakes falling."

I would sit on an airplane, not knowing how to begin to write in the book I had started a few years later—a true "memoir" that later was published as *Trust Your Heart*—and I would pick up Ira's book, *The Practice of Process Meditation,* and I would read a few paragraphs even, and they would give me courage and I would plunge into the writing, and my fear, and the block from writing, would evaporate.

I think this is because Ira was a gifted teacher, but he was also a spiritual healer. His teaching was deeply rooted in a belief that we each have to write our own bible, that creative life is a harnessing to the life force of the universe, like a lift from a higher power, the transforming of the inner into the outer.

Having creativity in your mind and in your heart at all times is exciting and scary. It is sometimes like living on the edge of a glacier that might move, or a river that might flood, or a mountain that might avalanche. Bravery comes when you need it, to do things that are forbidden, say things that may upset others; to put things on paper; to tell secrets.

When we tell the truth if we are writing memoir, we may be afraid of what those in our families may think, of what the world may think. We have to get beyond the family prohibitions, the danger signs, the feelings of shame in front of our friends, or in front of society. They cannot matter to us, not in any real way, not in any way that may interfere with the stories we have to tell, the songs we have to sing. I learned to write out all I could; to save the editing for later!

> My life sometimes had the qualities of a glacier. Movement was so slow as to be invisible, as though a ballet were being done under the water of a still lake. People about me walked and talked. They were festivals of activity. They appeared to have had a thaw in their glaciers, a flood that had cleared canyons where now vegetation thrived, thickets of scarlet and white flowers blossomed.

I curled cautiously underwater, daring to breathe as little as possible, frantic in my plunges to the surface to gulp air, slide back and resume a pose conducive to glacial progress and underwater breathing. I surfaced through the ice or through the water. Sometimes crystals fell around my shoulders or boats sank with the weight of jewels. I collected with a net, or with an ice pick, the personnel. When I came up to breathe for an instant, or spiked through the hard edge of ice, there might be a girl in a torn dress with blood running into the ground from a sword wound; a figure of a man riding away on horseback, his voice laughing from under a dusty Stetson; three women with sapphire crowns moving through the arc of a dungeon's mouth from black light into sunlight, their skirts billowing forward, and one Queen remaining in the shadows behind, her face white and her wrists wrapped in chains; one gypsy, who could dance as though on point, came whirling through the forest into a clearing, and was followed by a woman with bare feet who had thrown away her shoes and her infant and her fortune, and wished only that all should remain as it was at this moment, in this clearing; gale storms hit the cheeks of men on ships while the sails burst with wind and water above their heads; virgins lost their hearts and had their hair pinned to the ground by thieves in masks that made them look like mountain goats, or shadows.

In 1977, "Send in the Clowns" became a top-ten hit for the second time. I was thriving, succeeding, and on the brink of great successes.

During these past very very good years, things have happened to me that have been wonderful, and some that have been terrifying and unspeakable. I have tried to write about all of them, the wonderful and the incomprehensible.

I had to write about the death of my son, Clark, in part that I might live through it. The books and the songs that I have written about his death and his life and my own journey with him are something I had to do to help myself live through the tragedy; they are also what I can give other suicide survivors as a piece of the map they will need to overcome the terror of being a suicide survivor. Stephen Levine, poet, writer, and philosopher, says in *Meetings at the Edge*: "Most people who die leave a skeleton in their closet. The suicide leaves a skeleton in your closet."

Ed Shneidman, who started the suicide prevention movement in this country and has written dozens of books on suicide, says the suicide leaves a psychological skeleton that must be exhumed, examined, and processed by those who survive his or her death.

My beautiful son was thirty-three and had been sober for almost seven years. He and I had a close and loving relationship, which had been won at a great cost to both of us. His father and I had divorced when he was four, and I had lost custody when

Clark was five. He went to live with his father and they moved to Vancouver, British Columbia, from Connecticut. His father was a Blake scholar and a very bright, interesting man. But divorce had made us both bitter, and bitterness is catching. Still, when Clark came back to live with me when he was nine, we had the deep and close relationship that had been our treasure from the time he was born. He was his father's child, but he was mine as well, and emotionally we were always extremely good friends as well as mother and son.

I had been a mother since my son's birth, and now I was a single mother to a soon-to-be adolescent. He grew, got into trouble with drugs and alcohol, did wonderful things as well, and had a drug problem. No surprise, since I had the Irish Virus and it was certainly in the family.

But after many years of struggle, Clark got sober in 1984. I celebrated, and thanked God he had lived through his dark night of the soul. But the dark night's cousin was waiting around the corner.

When he died, I nearly lost my mind. No matter how close you come to the edge of the pit, you can always come closer, and I nearly fell in. The thing that held me back was the love of my family, my music, and my writing.

I wrote the books *Singing Lessons* and *Sanity & Grace* for me, and for his daughter, and for those who might be helped by hearing our stories. Sometimes we have to write and create for different reasons, sometimes for no reason we can name. The nameless call comes to us, the muse arrives at our door, having finished for the moment perhaps with, say, Leonard Cohen or the painter who lives next door. We must be ready to take orders, often whether we like them or not.

The songs I have written for Clark over the years sound through the tears and through the joys of my life as his mother, both during his life and during his absence from my life.

I lost you on a winter's day
In that cold city far away
A city by a river deep
With promises you could not keep
A place where you had gone to try
A place where you had longed to fly
A city smiling when you cried
A city sleeping when you died

Wings of angels tears of saints
Prayers and promises won't bring you back
Come to me in dreams again
Wings of angels tears of saints

In that cathedral by the hill
We stood and smiled in happier days
The fields along the river's edge
You fished and traveled hungrily

Your light burned in that sunny sky
Your voice above the water rang
I'd give it up give all I have
For one more chance to hear you sing

Wings of angels tears of saints
Prayers and promises won't bring you back
Come to me in dreams again
Wings of angels tears of saints

Child of thunder in the dark child whose voice was like a lark
Child whose spirits lifted hearts child of many beauties
When the birds flock to the south
When the wind calls to the north
You are in the falling snow
You are beauty going forth
You are heat and you are light
Sun above the mountain's peak
I would give the sun and moon
Once more just to hear you speak

Wings of angels tears of saints
Prayers and promises won't bring you back
Come to me in dreams again
Wings of angels tears of saints

—Judy Collins, "Wings of Angels"

Hard times can bring out the best in us, and force us to find the light, to reinvent ourselves, to face things that we would have chosen not to face. My struggles are my lessons, and are, I believe, carefully constructed to bring me the lessons I need to learn.

The struggle is the classroom of the soul,
the place we train to do what we would
not otherwise have done.

Chapter 16

Performing

*I*t's not enough to have talent," my friend George Furth says. "You have to have talent for talent."

I was born to perform, to get up in front of an audience; to love, be soothed by, and invigorated by live performance. Being in front of an audience makes my heart beat, my mind work, my eyes light up, and my soul soar. It is flying, it is feeling; it is being.

I have been performing concerts in the United States and other countries for more than four and a half decades now. I do fifty to seventy-five shows a year usually, and I feel privileged that I have been given such a great gift—and plan to go on until I drop. Performing, writing, recording, and singing are what I was born to do.

In the early years of my life, there was the piano, and there was singing, and performances on my father's radio show, at church or in school in the choir, or in plays. I sang "Someday My Prince Will Come" in the play *Cinderella* when I was twelve years old, had a job with Jack Blue's dance band in junior high school singing the standards, played a two-piano Mozart concerto with an orchestra when I was thirteen.

And then I found the guitar.

The songs I learned were, for me, the stories that would mold my journey. They were songs of love and fortune, of war and pity, and of pain, and, sometimes, even elation. I thought of myself primarily as a storyteller in the early years, and I used the lyrics to still an audience, to hush the mummers, to keep an auditorium or even a bar in Oklahoma so still you could hear a pin drop. I had watched my father leave an audience spellbound, often in tears, when he did his recitation of "Don Blanding's Dream House."

I wanted that magic connection to the audience, too. I met the performers who were guests on my father's radio show: George Shearing, Red Skelton, Bob Hope. If I couldn't be funny, I could make music. (I was playing the Mozart concerto when I met Shearing. After I began to play the guitar, George told me that it was a shame I had not continued playing classical music!! But I learned "Laura" from Shearing—that beautiful, haunting version that is a combination of classical and jazz that has probably influenced my writing of songs in the years since I first met him.

It was my goal to make clear to each and every person, from the front-row seats to the seats in the farthest corners of the auditorium, the nature of the story, the play of the words. I wanted to be heard, I meant to be heard, I HAD to be heard.

"Maid of Constant Sorrow," "The Greenland Fishery," "Tim Evans," "Anathea." Songs about work, the death penalty, the Greenland Fishery, on the stage of Carnegie Hall when I was twenty-three, a sprite of a girl in a short white dress, with a huge Martin guitar strapped across my middle; I was the opening act for Theodore Bikel, and I sang my heart out, songs that I had been singing in the clubs across the country: the Exodus in Denver, the Gilded Garter in Central City, L'Hibou in Ottawa, Gerde's Folk City in New York City. In smoky rooms where the booze flowed, in tidy clubs in Boston where the espresso flowed; I sang from petite stages or from huge expanses, like Carnegie, with all my might, all my soul, all my conviction.

I know a lot of the things you have to know; practicing, being ready, being on time—it's funny how being on time makes a difference to a performance. It is a good thing. On the other hand, I have gotten off planes or out of cars and walked right onto the stage and done wonderfully, but that is because I know how to be on time; being on time helps you handle being late.

The first solo concert I did in New York was at Town Hall. I was recording for Elektra Records by that time, and we were planning on recording the concert. One show, one chance, and it became an album I am proud of: *The Judy Collins Concert* from 1964. Jac Holzman's wife, Nina, who always threw wonderful parties for me upon the release of my albums, had a party for that concert, dinner at the Russian Tea Room, next door to Carnegie Hall. The day of the show, she called me in the morning and told me she had arranged for me to have a massage at Elizabeth Arden's, a couple of blocks away from Carnegie. I had my massage, then took a cab to the great hall, and sang, among other things, "Lord Gregory," "Bottle of Wine," "The Lonesome Death of Hattie Carroll." It was a thrilling concert. Every song was new, which was remarkable for a live concert, even in those days. We did a little fixing up in the studio, and that fall my fourth album on Elektra made its debut.

I have always liked making live concert albums, and have done many of them over the years. They have a sparkle and an excitement that, for the life of me, I can never seem to match in the studio, although there are moments of performance in the studio which are exciting and bring a timelessness to a song—I am thinking of "Send in the Clowns," "Both Sides Now," "The Blizzard." Actually, you are performing, whether you are on a stage or in a recording studio, and have to have the same feeling of excitement and wonder at what you are doing. But the stage is the place where stars are born, stars are in your eyes, stars are in the sky, somewhere, at night, and it is the magic of the stage that makes the mark of an artist, in the end. If you can do it on a stage, in ethereal space of the proscenium arch, you can do it anywhere.

As I sang, I let the story, and then the voice, carry the force of my love for the music in the stillness. I yearned to be heard, to be understood. I have to fly; there is no falling, not from here. No way out but out, onto the stage. Nothing beating but my heart; nothing showing but my heart.

I have been getting onto a stage from the time I was four and my father encouraged me to join him in singing "I'll Be Home for Christmas." I don't remember being frightened then, only terribly excited, so that I could hear my heart beat under my dress with the puckered bodice and the lace around the collar, a dress my mother had made for me; so excited I begged and pleaded with my father to let me sing in public again—on his radio show, in the little concerts that my piano teachers loved to have to show off their best pupils—I *longed* to be the best student! And later, at assemblies at school, in solos with the school choir, with the church choir, in the opera choruses that Dr. Brico needed singers for. "Andiam, andiam!" I sang in a high, bright, untrained teenaged soprano. And I loved the clothes that were required for performance.

They were special, made by my mother, exotic blue "squaw" dresses, with silver "rickrack," we called it, on the borders. And then there were the troubadour pants and long silk shirt I chose to perform in when I first starting singing with the guitar, telling my stories to audiences of college graduates in the smoky bars and folk clubs of the early sixties. I was comfortable, where I belonged, doing what I was meant to do. All I had to do was find other songs to sing—not just "I'll Be Home for Christmas!"

Somehow, as a child and a teenager, I didn't connect all of this pleasure and excitement with making a living. In 1950, in Denver, teachers and friends were not talking about careers after high school, although many of my friends, like me, studied music or dance or the arts seriously. But we were young women, and there was an unspoken agreement that we might be talented but that marriage, and families, was our future, not a career onstage. Certainly not the stage!

For all the performing I have done, there are still moments of sheer terror, where the blood runs hot and the skin is pale as ice, and you think, What am I doing? They are going to slaughter me! I am not going to survive this! I forget the words, or, worse, make up others on the spot! (I have been, at times, in favor of this, forgetting the lyrics to a song I have sung for years—always on television, in front of millions, not just a few folks at a private party! And making up words that, somehow, though they don't make any sense, always rhyme.)

Most people I have met have some degree of nervous tension about performing. The trick is not to let it stand in your way. The ice-in-the-veins moments before going onstage—or sometimes for days before a very special, unique concert, say, at Carnegie Hall, or a big television appearance—still happen to me sometimes; sheer terror, as though I am standing at the top of a cliff and don't know how I am going to make it down.

I am always surprised by feeling this infrequent possession, the chills creeping up my spine, my stomach in a knot. I could not eat, not if my life depended on it. I think, This is not professional, and yet I have talked to professionals who have enjoyed great fame and success who throw up before and after going onstage.

Laurence Olivier, in his sixties and after many years as a totally successful actor, became inexplicably terrified of going up on his lines, and suffered agonies when he had to go onstage, after having spent his life there. One actor I know must walk three times around the table in his dressing room; another clutches a cross; yet another, a crystal necklace. One has to have a shot of whiskey, another a bar of chocolate. And then there's the actor who must have tea with lemon, and spit three times in a row, before taking the stage. Many performers I knew in the sixties thought drugs were the answer; others swore by yoga and meditation.

For me, nerves don't happen often, but they *do* happen.

In the early seventies, I began to have trouble with my voice, and there ensued years of concern about singing—I would go on two-week silences to protect the instrument, so that I could sing. I went to doctors; I talked about the problem with my coach, Max. In 1977, my doctor finally told me that I would have to have surgery, a new laser technique that he said he could not guarantee would cure the problem—an enlarged capillary on the vibrating surface of my left vocal cord. I know now the problems were probably caused by drinking.

I had the surgery—straddling the fear that it might not fix the problem, but that if I didn't go through with it, I would not be able to sing anyway. I awoke with the conviction that everything was going to be all right, and my voice began to improve and repair soon, as I put everything I had ever learned from Max about singing to work. Still, the fear didn't leave me completely for three or four years.

I was lucky. I don't know what I would have done if I had not been able to sing. But I was, lucky, blessed, and I stopped drinking soon after the surgery. I bless my ENT, Dr. Don Weissman, every day of my life.

We all have physical impediments we have to deal with. The late-onset asthma that I have battled, and, to a great extent, conquered, was another phantom on the path of my career that threatened, when I couldn't sing because of it, to stop me from my work. Dancers and athletes have serious physical problems all during their careers. Jacques d'Amboise, the great dancer from the New York City Ballet, had his toes fused so that he could continue to dance into his fifth and sixth decade. Skiers break bones, have them set, and go back to ski the mountains again and set records. I have seen skiers with no legs who soar down the Colorado mountains, and others who can't see making their silken way down the slopes. Physical problems can be overcome, with the right passion and the right training, and, of course, with luck. And I am always reminded of my father's blindness, that it never stopped him from doing anything.

Perhaps luck is the most important attribute of all.

The more you do what you love—writing your poems, publishing books, getting into that first little regional magazine, then the collections, then selling your first story, or doing your first solo concert at Carnegie Hall, as I did in 1964—the more the thrill of the process is leavened, from time to time, with sheer terror. Who am I to be doing this? What do I think I am doing? What will the audience think? What will the critics say? The friends, the family?

There is good cause for this terror at times. There are bad reviews to contend with when we go public with our passions. There are critics who will blast us, or, worse, define us for ever and ever in a review in a newspaper or magazine; define us in terms that never seem to evaporate, no matter how often we try to remind reviewers, and readers, that we do not write *only* romance novels, or that we do not sing *only* arias; that we are writers, not *simply* of protest songs, but that we do other kinds of songs as well. That we are not *just* beatniks, or folk-singers, or art singers (my favorite niche: a sort of "You're so unique, you will never have an audience except for smart, sub-tle, intelligent people like me, and there are so few of us!"), but as singers, or writers, or painters, or whatever it is we do.

The frequency with which critics and interviewers alike reach for catchphrases and categories can be alarming, but it must not dissuade us. When people ask me what kind of music I sing, I like to say I sing Judy Collins songs. But this is just ju-venile, I suppose, and there is nothing to do but swallow your resentments and keep rewriting your biography, to no avail; after your first big public break, where you are defined, peo-ple think they know what you do, and will remind you of it no matter how you squirm, no matter how you yearn to coun-teract their categories.

Categories, after all, make you easier to sell. Just relax and enjoy it, I tell myself!

One of those chilling moments came at the pre-inauguration concert for President Bill Clinton. There were stars and su-perstars in the old sports facility outside the Beltway. The tel-evision cameras were roaming the audience; everyone who was anyone and could get a ticket was there: Barbra Streisand was in the next dressing room; Michael Jackson arrived with an en-tourage; many political friends were either singing or listening, and I was terrified. It had nothing to do with not knowing the words, or with the company—I knew the then governor of

Arkansas, having met him as well as Hillary in the previous year's campaign, when they came to see me and declared that I was better than ever; the governor had said in *People* magazine that, if elected, he would have a parade and have Judy Collins sing; he and Hillary had said they had named their daughter, Chelsea, after my version of "Chelsea Morning"; everything was fine, my dress fit, and I was thin, as thin as I usually only feel in my mind; no, I was simply wilting with anxiety. I had been singing well, for years, after my surgery, but the thought of a live camera was almost too much.

Television cameras on, I stepped onto the stage, and all fear dropped from my heart and I was fine. The feeling that I was going to die, only not in the future, left me. Instead of shivering in fear, I experienced glorious joy as I sang "Amazing Grace" with the Philander Smith College choir. I didn't miss words; I didn't flub the ending or miss notes. It was heaven.

For two decades, I did a solo concert at Carnegie Hall every year during the holidays, and for two decades, a week before the concert, I would get a terrible cold and be in fear of my very livelihood that I would not be able to sing. I always did. Sing. And probably no one in that beautiful hall knew that I had been in deep despair and hiding behind the flu for a week, terrified of the upcoming performance.

I don't have to do that anymore.

Most often, I perform joyously, with no apprehensions, no feeling of anxiety, no fears. Singing is what I do, and I feel I am always learning about it; it is a craft that keeps revealing new dimensions to me. In the past twenty years, I think my skills have grown, my confidence expanded. I keep performing, through the anxieties, through the days and years of my life.

If you are a performing artist, or a writer who will have to read your books in bookstores, on television, at public appearances, you have to learn how to perform. If you are a sculptor and have to present your slides, you have to learn how best to do that. You can take public-speaking courses to help you sell your art, talk about yourself and your work. Learning what NOT to do is as important as learning what TO do. Classes in speaking, reading to an audience, acting, making a public presentation of your work, will always help you in ways you might not see at first.

Getting over self-consciousness about what you do before the public is an all-important part of your work. You have done the preparation work, the writing, the painting, the practicing, the creation of new songs, new prose, new painting, and now the performance—whether you are a singer or a dancer or a painter or a chef—must be learned. Performance is the next step, the continuity, if you will, of your creativity.

Of course, there are degrees of skill required. I was born and trained to be a performer, yet I still work with coaches, teachers, critics, my friends, and my audiences, who teach me always how to better what I am doing.

Writers must often learn to read in public, do interviews,

face television cameras, and, more often, radio microphones and interviewers. All of us sometimes have to have nerves of steel, and actors, singers, musicians, performers often must overcome the great burden of stage fright to do their work.

There are things to do for this fear, of course, and many people have remedies, habits developed over years. Mine is simple, and very much akin to the things we talked about in the first chapter: habits; things I do every time I perform; rituals, you might call them, ceremonies of the offstage world that make the onstage world work. When I perform, I arrive at the venue usually three and a half hours before the concert. I do a microphone check with my sound engineer and my musical director, and play a few songs, getting used to the stage and to the hall. I test the sound. I walk around the stage, getting the feel for it.

I have dinner. I meditate. I shower. I am quiet. I bless the audience. Then I sing.

When I was drinking, I never moved from the front of the microphone. I sang with my eyes tightly shut, usually unable to look out at the audience, in a sort of stunned, dreamlike trance. I didn't move on the stage, and had no sense of what the rest of the space on the stage was about.

I seldom talked to my audiences then. I had very little to say; I was just trying to remember lyrics, to go into a trance, to stay focused. As the freedom I had as a performer began to dawn on me, I started talking to the audience, and some wished I would just shut up! I recall jokes, I invent jokes; I talk about what I am doing, what I am feeling.

Now I have a great time with my audiences. The lyrics that I sing are terribly important, but, as the years have gone by, the banter and spontaneous sharing with the audience has become a source of pleasure and joy to me. I love my audiences, and feel there is a shared experience going on with them when I perform.

If I don't know the words as well as I would like, I can feel as though I am being put through the veritable wringer, the same kind of wringer I caught my arm in when I was a nine-year-old, doing the laundry in the basement with the old-fashioned washing machine. My first symphony concert (and last, until I began doing concerts with symphony orchestras, with and without guitar), playing the Mozart concerto with Dr. Brico's orchestra in Denver, was memorable for the nerves that preceded it. It was my singing teacher, Max, who often told me that to alleviate the nerves, one should simply concentrate on the piano, or the lyrics, or the words, if you are reciting poetry, or the character, if you are acting in a play or a movie. Still, all the concentration in the world, all the meditation, all the clarity, cannot always stop that terrifying, free-flying, almost electric feeling I get once every few years that someone has poured antifreeze into my lungs and it is not working.

Chilling—

And worth every moment.

I have heard performers say that *unless* they feel that terror before every performance, the performance will not be as good as it could be. I don't feel it all the time, which is all the more reason to be horrified when the antifreeze act begins before a concert I am fairly certain about. It can come on me if I know you are in the audience, a friend, a famous peer. Please don't tell me who is in the audience, I once heard Barry Humphries tell his assistant, who should have known him better by then, before one of his astonishing performances as Dame Edna.

It can happen to all of us.

The thing is not to clutch, not to faint, not to leave the theater, not to call in psychotic when you feel this way, but to try to go with the flow, and *use* the antifreeze in whatever way you can. There is a priceless payoff when you face this fear and get out there, whatever it is that you are doing—singing, dancing, reading your poetry, reading from your most recent book, showing your paintings to a new gallery. The fear is energy in disguise. And it's a way to keep the population down, I suppose, so that there will not be too many performers and not enough audiences. Also, I think you have to love what you do enough to go through these trip-to-the-dentist, minor-surgery kind of fears, and come out the other side. (I heard recently that "minor surgery" is what happens to someone else.)

An audition can do it.

I auditioned once for a part in an Arnold Schwarzenegger movie, *Junior;* I have done some, though not a lot of, acting, and a friend who was the movie's co-producer convinced the director that I would be a great "off-beat" choice for the part of the head of a pregnancy spa where Arnold goes in his ninth month. A surprise, with a payoff of some sort. The nerves began after I did the first cold reading in New York City, on a lark, really—I thought for sure I would simply be treated to a few smiles and nods and go home, knowing I would not be considered for the part. When I got the callback, the nerves began—although I had a fabulous experience doing the movie, out in California's Carmel Valley, at a mansion set in the soft, Italian-looking hills, doing scenes and having meals with Arnold and Danny DeVito, and getting to know Emma Thompson and her mother; in many scenes, I was a nervous wreck.

Every day, I would see Arnold cavorting with his kids, and he would sing with me, asking me to play his favorite song, "The Blizzard," under the arching roof of the mansion's main hall. He would come in after his run, or his golf game or his bike ride, striding quickly across the room, a cigar clenched in his teeth, unlighted in deference to his wife, Maria, and all of us nonsmokers. He told me that when he had immigrated to the United States, I was the first person he had heard in concert, at the Civic Center in Santa Monica. I liked him enormously.

Some of my scenes with Arnold were easy and fun, and others, for no reason that I could fathom, were terrifying. The nervousness would come out of nowhere, but I got through it, somehow, and got to know Arnold a little bit in the bargain.

There have been other films and stage appearances, of course. I sang and acted in *Peer Gynt,* in 1969, in which I played Solveig to Stacy Keach's Peer Gynt; in *Christy,* the series based on the Catherine Marshall books about a young woman who goes to a small village in Kentucky to teach Quaker children; and, for a couple of weeks, in *The Exonorated,* Bob Balaban's amazing stage production of the stories of six men and a woman who spent years on death row for crimes they didn't commit. I hope to do more work in film and on stage, and plan to launch a one-woman show sometime in the next year or two.

I am afraid that the chill of stage fright will not have made a disappearing act by then, however. I just think you have to get used to it, because the thrill of being present, when it is all going well, is priceless. I would not miss it for the world. I get an enormous feeling of elation and joy when I stand on stage and begin to sing. I am in the dark, usually, and the spotlight has caught me in my shiniest face, my best dress, my most glamourous pose, for I love to dress *up* when I sing. I love to look and feel as though I just stepped off the runway, out of the beauty salon; that I am performing a song that is new, or doing something that is unusual.

Know your lyrics. Know your words. Or make up lyrics of words that make sense!

"All the world's a stage, / And all the men and women merely players," as Shakespeare said. We all have our parts, and whether we are in front of or behind the curtains there are times when our actions and lives are public in some way.

I am truly blessed. I always wanted to be in front of the curtain, performing. I am grateful that I have been given that opportunity, and I feel that I have another half of my lifetime to devote to my art, to performance, to walking onto that stage and doing what I love the most: making music.

Chapter 17

Letting Go of Perfection

In the valleys you look for the mountains
In the mountains you search for the rivers
You have no where to go you are where you belong
You can live the life you dream
If you call him your master will find you
Seven bars on the gate will not hold him
Seven fires burning bright only give him delight
You can live the life you dream

All your treasure buys you nothing but the moment
All your poverty has lost you everything
Love will teach your dream . . . to sing
　　　　　　　—Judy Collins, "The Life You Dream"

Sometimes I have to forget what I think I know in order to have something come into my thoughts, my heart, that was blocked by always knowing. You know when something slips your mind, or you forget a word, and there is that space that opens up where the name you forgot is unimportant, the subject you wanted to talk about is gone, but there is a kind of sigh that the psyche emits—as though for once, for once, you forgot whatever it was that was so important, and that is a blessing. An angel passes, they say, in that silence, when the mind is quiet, when we can forget for a while why we think we are here, and perhaps just *be* here. To receive what comes to us.

> *And sometimes it is necessary to forget everything*
> *we ever learned and take that leap, out into the*
> *air, as though jumping out of an*
> *airplane, theoretically.*

Let go of the training wheels, plunge into the water, get to the edge of something and simply let go, knowing that 5 percent of inspiration is where the magic happens, and 95 percent, as my singing teacher Max used to tell me, is about technique. The 5 percent is what makes a Horowitz out of a person who does scales and exercises every day, and learns his pieces perfectly. The 5 percent is the spellbinding, the gripping, the intoxicating. The 5 percent is what art is all about.

When I was studying the piano, I often practiced two and a half hours at a time. My teacher was the great Antonia Brico, a taskmaster who wanted the best for me, and wanted me to become a concert pianist. I had the hands, she said, and could go far in the classical field.

When I memorized a concerto, like the Mozart two piano concerto I played when I was thirteen with Brico's orchestra in Denver, I hovered over the music, studying and learning. Brico's students were taught what she liked to call Memory by Analysis, which entailed studying each measure as it came, a page, sometimes a phrase, at a time. This amounted to the studying of theory and harmony, as it was necessary to understand each construction, by Mozart or, later, Rachmaninoff, in order to understand and have the mind remember what the entire piece was like. Brico's theory was that as we memorized in this way, we would never really lose the outline, the overall arch, of the piece.

I memorized my first Mozart concerto in 1952, in the backseat of the Buick "Claudia," as I sped with my family from Denver to Idaho to visit my great-grandfather Booth for what would turn out to be the last time. My parakeet, Chris, was in a cage hung from the ceiling of the Buick, the hooks to his cage secured at four corners. The cage swung on the curves of White Bird Pass, and the blue ball of fluff sang to the sound of the tires. On either side of me my brothers read or slept, while the cardboard keyboard spread out on my knees and my fingers sought the chords of the concerto and memorized the intricate moves between black and white keys. When we returned from the trip two weeks later, I had most of the concerto under my hands, and the rest of it in my mind.

My co-pianist, Danny Guerrero, now a successful bandleader and trumpet player in Los Angeles, and I began to spend long hours practicing for the big date in February 1952, when we would perform the concerto with Brico's orchestra. My mother got me a white organdy dress, and shoes to match. The chaos of my household settled down around the coming date and I practiced like mad, day in and day out, so that the performance would be perfect.

A few days before the performance, I was at my lesson with Dr. Brico. She listened as I played my piano part, and then she sat down beside me at the piano.

"Now," she said, "I want you to stop practicing and start thinking and listening." She had me skip an occasional day of practicing, which I had never been told to do, and never thought I could do—after all, the cardboard keyboard that traveled over four thousand miles in the backseat of the car was a testimonty that she wanted me to practice. Why would she tell me to let up?

But I could see the results almost immediately. I began to dream about the concerto, and to see it and feel it in different ways. The notes began to be lines of melody; the fingerings began to seep into my heart, as well as my mind. I was practicing, yes, but differently. I was learning to let go and fly.

☽

Also, letting go allows your mind to grasp something that is floating at the edges, as though in your pheripheral sight, just out of reach. Letting go lets things in that place to come in.

I have a technique for finding the songs that I sing, and I

suppose in a way there is nothing mysterious about it. Sometimes the song just jumps into my thoughts and my subconscious and stays, but often I prompt it by selecting a number of songs that appeal to me, playing them once, and then waiting. Sometimes it takes a few days, but suddenly while putting on my makeup or driving in a car or just before going to sleep, a melody will pop into my head like a flash of lightning. Aha! This is the one, out of all the others. And Iearn it, and that is that. Magic.

Sometimes the writing of a song is propelled by an event, a sight, a story, a sudden flash of an idea that spurs me to put it together so that, just as it did when I was sitting in the library as a child in Los Angeles, or listening to my father read to me from Melville, I can hear how the story ends. When I see that opening, have the shot of an inkling of something around a corner or just over the edge, behind the hill, or see something that strikes my imagination—like the fireman at the Roxy turning around so that I could see the tattoo on his neck, the number, 343, in black ink; his telling me that a "lot of the guys" have that tattoo—it keeps resonating in my imagination until I have to do it.

Sometimes, when I am praying and meditating and in the "groove" of my days, the time I thought I would need to do something simply evaporates.

Sometimes things take even longer than I think they will. It once took me five years to finish a song, "Che," about Che Guevara. On the other hand, I finished writing "Since You've Asked," my first song, in forty minutes.

You never know.

When I was fourteen my father insisted I play a very difficult piece called "La Campanella," by Franz Liszt, in public at a concert he was doing for a local trade fair in Denver. It was a very flashy and difficult piece, and though I had been memorizing it for months, I knew it would not be ready for a public performance.

In a total panic, not knowing what to do, where to turn, I took a bottle of pills. I wanted to die, intended to die, and did what I could to assure that I would, because I could not imagine the alternative.

Obviously, I lived through the experience.

I had to learn other ways to handle my demands for perfection, and other methods for dealing with my desire to see things done on my timetable. In later years, I would lose a son to suicide, and I know what a terrible thing it is to suffer such a loss.

I know part of my lesson here is that I can't always control the things that happen to me. Also, I have had to learn that it is not what happens to us, but what we do with the experience that is the real question. How I react to situations is the only thing over which I have any control in this unpredictable life we lead.

Perfectionism is thought by some to be a spiritual issue, and it can cause me to do self-punishing things, things that are not helpful but hurtful. Perfectionism certainly played a part in my wishes to self-destruct. And it has to be balanced, for none of us is God, but we must try to do the most perfect work we can.

I am pretty good at meeting publishing deadlines, and those for records. And of course, I have to be onstage at a certain time, and have never been late for a show that I know of, even when I was having a difficult travel day, but I make do, forgo the shower, get onstage in street clothes, anything to make sure the curtain goes up on time. So I do have a thing about getting under the wire with my time limits, and it may feel like perfectionism to others around me, sending something back to be done a different way, redoing a song in a recording studio. My co-producer may think I am nuts because I want to hear something differently, but it is, after all, my voice, my recording, and I am the one who is going to have to live with it. Or not.

My husband, Louis Nelson, is an industrial designer. In the early nineties, he was commissioned to design the wall for the Korean Memorial Wall to be erected in Washington, D.C. For three years he worked on the creation of a piece of art that would be timeless and bring closure to those who had fought in that forgotten war, and when it was near completion and dedication, he began to write poetry about walls. I read his poetry and was inspired to write the song "Walls." It commemorates the Korean experience, I hope, but I think of it as a song about the hearts and souls of those who have to fight the wars we put them into, the cut of pain and the dreams of home, the determination that this will never, pray God, have to happen again if I give blood and bone.

Listen to my heart, look into my eyes
I have seen the stars falling from the skies
Listen to my fears, yours will lift and fly
Let me show you where, I have touched the air
Stories from the past, each as true as mine
We can speak at last through the sands of time
We are not forgotten anymore

These are things I know, trampled fields of snow
Sheets of falling rain, hope that concurs pain
Souls that call again in my memory
Through the veils of light falling on the sea
Letters wrapped in love, lips pressed in my dreams
Holy thoughts and brave, men who laugh and weep

We are not forgotten anymore
I am the face on the wall
Spirit of hope ever rising
I am the prayer in your heart for peace

Letting go of what I think should be perfect will let me find the thing as it is meant to be. I "should" have had the perfect time to write that song—say, a year? Instead, I had to let go of my preconceived notions and take what came. In that moment of letting go, I found a new voice and a new friend, whom I will treasure even though he is not here in the flesh anymore. My perfectionism might even stand in my way of accepting simply his spirit, and insist I see him in the flesh, thereby missing the spirit. Perfectionism, then, might well be seen as a lack of faith.

Let go of perfection and reach for faith.

Succeeding

W hat is success?

Is it financial abundance? Is it how many books you sell? How many records you sell? Is it having your paintings and your art in the right gallery, and an audience that appreciates your work and keeps buying everything that comes out, year after year?

Is it having great reviews, standing ovations, a crowd at every backstage door?

How do you count the success in your life? Do you count it in financial ways? Emotional ways? Do you think you have been successful if you get what you want?

How do you feel if you don't get what you want?

Do you feel you have failed?

I have had many kinds of success in my life. My career has had its ups and downs, over a period of forty-five years. In the first eleven, I had a recording career with a major company, Elektra, in which I was part of the building of the company, at the start of what my brother Denver calls the "great folk scare." I had support for my albums and a constant feeling that my work was not only understood, but also loved and cherished.

After 1972, Elektra's management changed, and its point of view toward the artists it represented changed. For a few years, the resonance of the first few years was maintained. In 1984, after nearly twenty-four years of recording for Elektra, we parted, and there followed a series of recordings I made for various labels: Telstar in the UK, and then Gold Castle, Sony, Geffen, Mesa Blue Moon, and Elektra again in the late nineties, when I did a compilation as well as a new Christmas album for the company at which I had spent my first successful, satisfying years.

I found it heartbreaking to search, every other year or so, for another record company that I hoped could fulfill my expectations. I kept trying, and I kept recording and doing concerts all over the world, building. But the experience of hearing the promises of many recording executives and seeing the results, which many times fell far short of both the obvious business ideals as well as my own expectations, made me ready to take an enormous risk, financially as well as artistically, and start my own record label, with all the benefits and pitfalls of doing so.

I wouldn't have had the courage to do this without the feelings of total failure that preceded my decision to take my own professional direction in my hands. I share this because the illusion for many people is that a career is a straight line from start to exciting, successful finish, for anyone who has had a long and seemingly successful career. And the truth is, there are always ups and downs; there are always difficult decisions, and people do not always do things the way I would like them to.

If I can get the work in, and do my best, and reach my personal goals of being creative, I feel successful. I don't let other people dictate the way I feel about my own success.

Today I think of success as doing my part.

Chapter 19

Praying

> *Yet she, singing upon her road,*
> *Half lion, half child, is at peace.*
> —W. B. Yeats, "Against Unworthy Praise"

They say that praying is talking to God and meditation is listening. I have to talk, and I have to listen, in order to go forward.

Sometimes I find myself just walking along, talking to myself, praying for God's will, not my own, to supersede all my plans. I have a lot of plans, always have. Too few plans is not my problem, too many plans is also not my problem, because what is meant to happen, I believe, will happen no matter what I do.

I find prayer comforting and the walking prayer releases my mind from obsessing on what is not exactly right and about what I know is wrong and could be easily fixed, if, as my sister often says, God were paying attention. But I pray on, because I cannot do otherwise. I find my anchor and my confidence is in prayer. I am sustained, and uplifted by prayer.

Prayer is so individual, and every way you pray is the right way, the way for you, as the way I pray is totally right for me. I believe that. It sustains me, and we believe in what sustains us, and gives us hope.

Emerson said that "one should strive for an original relationship with the universe," and I suppose that my wandering, troubadour, singing life is just that. It is certainly different!

For in the travels through the world, among the lakes and the mountains, through the airports and over the highways of the Great Continent, I dream and write my songs and poems and journals; I sing my songs and find audiences that listen and take my journeys with me. A unique kind of homage to the land, where my hopes spring to life, and the air I breathe, the sights I see, in this perpetual traveling I do, like the circuit riders of old, measuring the miles in dreams. Creating the life I have to have to survive.

When I sing life is pure and simple. Singing heals; I know it does.
It has healed me. Singing is like a spiritual sauna: The lungs are
working and the mind is going and the mouth and heart are en-
gaged in a process of exportation and pleasure. When I am
singing, I am completely concentrated, and although I can think
of other things, I am in a world of my own, removed from any
stress. No one can harm me. I cannot be angry or intolerant or
thinking of revenge or of negative things. Sometimes, if I feel like
screaming, I can sing instead. Singing is like a meditation that
flows, uninterrupted, during which the voice, it seems to me,
mends the soul—of the singer and of the listener. The "other"
becomes melted into the "many" in singing; the many become as
one; the "different" have understanding of one another; the half-
hearted become whole, pure.

The voice of the singer, heard by the listener, combines the dreams
and the thoughts of those who are listening. There is a kind of
mystical bridge that forms between the audience and the singer,
and on this bridge our hearts are healed.

—Judy Collins, *Singing Lessons*, 1997

Prayer helps us be warriors. The creative act is one of great
boldness where you act on your own beliefs. Creativity is the
ability to risk being different from the crowd, to think differently, to act differently, and yet in a calculated, orderly fashion
so that your idea, your vision, your new insight, is clear. It is
the successful effort to make completeness out of chaos, to

make the world dance, for a moment or forever, to your drum, at your pace, to your dream.

I try to pray before I work.

There is much about prayer and meditation in the art of being creative. In fact, the creative life is a spiritual life, and, as Yogananda says, "The spiritual path is like a razor's edge. It is not simple at all. Seclusion is the price of greatness . . . when I am alone I am with God."

I wake in Oklahoma; the sun is coming up through the curtains of the Renaissance Hotel, sort of in between a Four Seasons and a Holiday Inn. "Where the sun comes sweeping down the plains," rolls through my mind. What a line! What a song! I was raised on all those songs, songs Daddy sang while he shaved, while he got ready for the day, for his radio show. While he got ready for the fight not to take that first drink that day.

I push the button on the coffeemaker in the bathroom. The great romance of being a singer and writer on the road, songwriter, singer, writer, is the little things. I pour a cup of coffee and it steams in the cup as the sun slants yellow across the room. I throw a scoop of designer protein into a glass from the plastic pouch I carry, and add a packet of Splenda and bottled water from the minibar that is cleared at each hotel I stay in, of everything but the waters and the diet Cokes and the booze. I don't mind the booze, it doesn't tempt me, I don't fight the drink anymore. But the crackers, cashews, pistachios, jelly beans, chocolates stamped with the name of the hotel, pretzels covered in chocolate, yogurt-covered raisins! I fight them, so they were cleared out before I checked in yesterday.

So glad I do not drink today. Those days on the road before sobriety are like a nightmare dream, a landscape filled with skeletons of pain and, often, humiliation. As someone said,

I like to have a martini,
Two at the very most.
After three I'm under the table,
After four I'm under my host!
—Attributed to Dorothy Parker

But not anymore. Living a bit like a monk, I stir my protein drink and gulp coffee. This morning I won't have time to read my meditation books—Emmet Fox, *Each Day a New Beginning, One Day at a Time*—so I stuff them back into my suitcase, along with the boots from last night, the shirt that I threw across the room with the boots before I fell into bed and into a deep sleep after a day of traveling from New York, singing a concert, and getting to my hotel to work out while watching a movie on TV. The workout clothes are there, too, and the nightgown I tore off when I was creaming my makeup off and brushing my teeth.

An hour does it, as the heat increases and I throw the switch on the wall to cool and the fan to high. I do my morning meditation while I put on makeup, breathing in, breathing out, counting to twenty and then going through the morning prayers that carry me from town to town, from Oklahoma to Denver this morning, and from morning to night in the years of days I have traveled the world, a troubadour with a caffeine habit and a passion for making music and writing in journals and playing the piano, for colors and dark nights when it rains and I can hear the sound of birds hiding in the trees. It has been a fight to evolve from a singer who was trained to be a pianist and became a performing artist, to get permission from my self and my inner demons and critics, to go on with the things that I felt in my heart, and live a life that is all about creativity.

In my meditations I pray for my family and for abundance; I bless the people I know who are ill or suffering some difficult times in their lives. I pray for my husband and for my Persian cat, who climbed into my suitcase, as she usually does, when I was packing to leave yesterday. I pray for my son, for my brothers and sister, my mother and father and stepfather, for my granddaughter. I thank God for my health, my voice. I think of what my friend George Furth told me—it's never too late to have a sparkling future. I pray for my friends; "It's called friendship. It's like therapy for free." I have a little money, and I'm grateful for my friends. They know all my secrets.

I thank God for diet Coke and protein bars, for concerts and concert promoters, for airplanes and the TSA; for the apples in the basket on the registration desk at the hotel, for hot soup at Boston's Legal Sea Foods; for soft pretzels (Jenny's) and roasted half chickens (anybody's). I thank God for my singing teacher, Max, and my love of music, songs, singers, writers. I thank God I practiced the piano when I was young and that I learned to type when I was pregnant. I thank God for my apartment in New York, where I have written songs and books and watched the sun set over the Hudson River. I pray for songs, for poems, for writing to come to me today; I pray to find the right songs for the new album. I pray to write new songs, and write new prose. I am starting a book on creativity soon, and I would like to think I am still, after all these years, creative.

I wrestle into my clothes and call for a bellhop. And I am on my way—again.

Prayer for the Creative Life

God, give me the strength to be surrendered,
    to be open to what the day brings
Give me gratitude and hope
    and lead me to the places I need to go—
Bless my uncertainty with curiosity
My searching with calm
Bless my action with release
Let my heart be open, my mind clear
Let my muse be nearby, not always at
    Leonard Cohen's house—
Bless Leonard Cohen
Let me see beyond the obvious
And hear the serenade of the present
In the silence of the moment
Let me reach for harmony
Let me learn the melody, and forget nothing
Let me be simple but precise
Let me feel confident and eager
Release me from fear and negativity
Show me the path
And give me courage to travel it, one day at a time

SONGS BY JUDY COLLINS THAT APPEAR IN *MORNING, NOON, AND NIGHT*:

"Fallow Way," from *Forever . . . The Judy Collins Anthology* (Elektra, 1997)

"The Life You Dream," from *Sanity & Grace* (Delta Music, 1989)

"Trust Your Heart," from *Voices* (Clarkson Potter/Publishers, 1995)

"The Blizzard (The Colorado Song)," from *All on a Wintry Night* (Wildflower Records, 2000)

"Since You've Asked," from *Wildflowers* (Elektra, 1967)

"Houses," from *Judith* (Elektra, 1975)

"Song for Sarajevo," from *All on a Wintry Night* (Wildflower Records, 2000)

"Kingdom Come," from *Judy Collins Wildflower Festival* (Wildflower Records, 2001)

"Wings of Angels," from *The Essential Judy Collins* (Wildflower Records, 2004)

"Walls (We Are Forgotten)," from *Forever . . . The Judy Collins Anthology* (Elektra, 1997)

PERMISSIONS

"The Life You Dream" by Judy Collins

"Houses" by Judy Collins

"Since You've Asked" by Judy Collins

"The Blizzard (The Colorado Song)" by Judy Collins

"Trust Your Heart" by Judy Collins

© 1987 by Universal Music Corporation on behalf of itself and Wildflowers Co./ASCAP

"The Fallow Way" by Judy Collins

© 1988 by Universal Music Corporation on behalf of itself and Wildflowers Co./ASCAP

"Kingdom Come" by Judy Collins

© 2001 by Wildflowers Co./ASCAP

ABOUT THE AUTHOR

Judy Collins is truly the definition of a living legend. From the time she discovered folk music and was signed to Elektra Records in 1961 to her current new albums, songs, books, television specials, and work with UNICEF and land mines, Judy has always remained creative and vibrant as an artist. She has enjoyed forty-five illustrious years in the public eye, filled with more than forty albums, numerous top-ten hits, Grammy nominations, and gold- and platinum-selling albums.

In April 2005, Judy's independent label, Wildflower Records, will release her long-awaited new album, *Portrait of an American Girl*, the first Judy Collins studio album in nearly a decade.

The author of *Sanity & Grace: A Journey of Suicide, Survival, and Strength*, *Trust Your Heart*, *Singing Lessons*, *Voices*, *Amazing Grace*, *The Judy Collins Songbook*, and the novel *Shameless*, she lives in New York City with her husband, Louis Nelson.